Janice VanCleave's
Math for Every Kid

Easy Activities that Make Learning Math Fun

Janice VanCleave

John Wiley & Sons, Inc.

New York • Chichester • Brisbane • Toronto • Singapore

Dedicated to a special friend and
wonderful math teacher, Nancy Rothband

Illustrated by Barbara Clark

Library of Congress Cataloging-in-Publication Data

VanCleave, Janice Pratt.
   [Math for every kid]
   Janice Van Cleave's math for every kid : easy activities that make learning math fun / by Janice Van Cleave.
      p.   cm. — (Janice VanCleave's Science for Every Kid Series)
   Includes index.
   Summary: Presents 101 simple math problems and experiments intended to introduce basic mathematical principles.
   ISBN 0-471-54693-3 (lib. ed.) — ISBN 0-471-54265-2 (pbk.)
   1. Mathematics—Juvenile literature. [1. Mathematics.]
I. Title. II. Title: Math for every kid. III. Series.
QA39.2.V35   1991
510—dc20   91-10302

Printed in the United States of America

20 19 18 17 16 15

Preface

This is a basic math book designed to teach facts, concepts, computational skills, and problem-solving strategies. Math is a part of our everyday life; each section introduces math concepts in a way that makes learning useful and fun.

English and metric units are given for all problems involving measurement. The objective is not to teach conversions between the two systems of measurement, but to give comparable examples using both systems. Exact conversions are not always used; when possible, numbers are rounded to the nearest whole number. For example, although 4 inches = 10.16 centimeters, 4 inches = 10 centimeters is used in this book.

The introductory Purpose for each section defines the concept that will be introduced.

Facts giving definitions and explanations of terms and symbols to be used are listed before the Problem is given.

The Problem contains a question or situation requiring the facts. A Solution using step-by-step examples is provided along with detailed diagrams.

An Exercise with practice problems for each section provides an opportunity for readers to develop their skills. The problems move from easy to more difficult. An asterisk in the left margin indicates activities requiring the highest level of math skills.

An Activity in each section allows the reader to apply the specific skill taught to problem-solving situations in the real world.

v

Answers for the Exercises are given at the end of each section with step-by-step instructions for solving the problems.

This book was written to make the learning of math skills a fun experience and thus encourage the desire to investigate topics involving math in greater depth and with less trepidation.

Contents

Introduction

Math is a special language using numbers and symbols to study the relations existing between quantities. This book deals with the study of measurements, graphs, geometric figures, and problem solving. A foundation of basic math facts is essential for everyone. Questions such as How much?, How far?, or How many? are part of everyday living. Understanding measurements can provide the skills needed for finding the answers to such questions. This book will make you more comfortable with the mathematics you deal with daily and provide a few basic tools to open doors leading to more mathematical discoveries.

From the Egyptian papyrus scrolls, the oldest forms of recorded history, we learn that as far back as 4000 B.C. numbers and mathematics were important. The first calendar required a system of numbering, as did recording the movements of celestial bodies. These early people laboriously counted with their fingers. Elementary-school children today quickly solve problems with inexpensive hand-held calculators. Are all the math secrets known? No. Mathematics is a living, growing science. The more we learn, the better the tools produced, and, with better tools, more questions arise. The science of math is a never-ending quest with a constant reward of new math skills. Measuring that first-caught fish or the success of baking a cake is a steppingstone to the future reward that mathematical skills can bring.

This book makes mathematics a simple language, one that you can easily understand and use. It is designed to teach math concepts in such a way that they can be applied to many similar situations. The problems, experiments, and other application activities were selected for their ability to be explained in basic terms with little complexity. One of the main objectives of the book is to present the FUN of mathematics.

Read each section carefully and follow each procedure in order. It is suggested that the sections be read in order, as well. There is some buildup of information from the first to the last section. The pattern for each section is:

1. Objective: The goal for the section.
2. Facts: Definition and explanation of terms and/or symbols to be used.
3. Problem: A question or situation requiring the information in the Facts section.
4. Solutions: Step-by-step instructions for solving the problem.
5. Exercises: Practice problems for you to reinforce your skills.
6. Activity: A project to allow you to apply the specific skill taught to problem-solving situations in the real world.
7. Answers: Answers for Exercises with step-by-step instructions.
8. Glossary: All **bold-faced** terms are defined in a Glossary at the end of the book. Be sure to flip back to the Glossary as often as you need to, making each term part of your personal vocabulary.

General Instructions for Problem Section

1. Study each problem and solution carefully by reading them through once or twice.
2. Do the practice problems by following the same steps described in the solution section.
3. Check your answers to evaluate your work.
4. Redo the problem if any of your answers are incorrect. Start over and try again.

General Instructions for Activity Section

1. Read each activity completely before starting.
2. Collect needed supplies. You will have less frustration and more fun if all the necessary materials for the activities are ready before

you start. You lose your train of thought when you have to stop and search for supplies.

3. Do not rush through the activity. Follow each step very carefully, never skip steps, and do not add your own. Safety is of utmost importance, and by reading each activity before starting, then following the instruction exactly, you can feel confident that no unexpected results will occur.

4. Observe. If your results are not the same as described in the activity, carefully reread the instructions, and start over from step one.

Acknowledgments

I want to thank a group of students from Crockett, Texas, who helped me test and refine a number of the procedures and exercises. We worked together to ensure that only fully tested, workable problems were included. Thank you: Meredith Clark, Katie Cunningham, Lauren Cocoros, John Holmes, Daniel Kelly, Mark Land, Troy Leland, Jennie Leland, Hugh Leland, Matt Roberts, and Laura Wilson. Tami Scruggs, math teacher at the Jordan School in Crockett, helped schedule our review sessions and worked with us from pie sections to glob!

I
Basics

1
Fractions

Purpose   To write fractions.

Facts   A fraction tells how many parts are in the whole and refers to a part of the total.

The pie is divided into 8 equal parts. Sue is eating one of the pie pieces. $1/8$ is the fraction that tells what part of the pie Sue is eating. When you read a fraction, say the top number first and then the bottom number. $1/8$ is read as one-eighth.

The top number of a fraction is called the **numerator** and tells how many of the equal parts of the whole are being considered. The bottom number is called the **denominator** and tells the total number of equal parts in the whole.

$$\frac{1}{8} = \frac{\text{numerator}}{\text{denominator}} = \frac{\text{Pieces of pie being eaten}}{\text{Total number of pie pieces}}$$

Problem

Question   What fraction of the total number of frogs are in the water?

Think!   How many frogs are in the water?   4
What is the total number of frogs present?   6
4 of the 6 frogs are in the water.

Answer   4/6 of the frogs are in the water.

Exercise

1. a. What fraction of the children are skating?
  b. What fraction of the children are playing marbles?

2. a. What fraction of the children are flying kites?
  b. What fraction of the children are sitting?

Activity: HALF-LIFE

Purpose   To demonstrate how radioactive materials change.

Materials   typing paper   marking pen
                2 empty shoe boxes   scissors
                timer

Procedure

- Use the marking pen to label one shoe box Changed and the other box Unchanged.
- Use the scissors to cut the sheet of paper in half.
- Place one of the paper halves in the box marked Unchanged.
- Place the second half piece of paper in the Changed box. All papers placed in the Changed box are to be left there, undisturbed, throughout the experiment.

- Set the timer for 1 minute.

- At the end of 1 minute, remove the paper from the Unchanged box and cut it in half.

- Separate the resulting pieces as before, placing one in the Changed box and one in the Unchanged box.

- Again set the timer for 1 minute.

- Continue to cut the piece of paper in the Unchanged box in half at the end of each minute until the paper becomes too small to cut. Always place one of the halves in the Changed box and the other in the unchanged box.

Results   At the end of 1 minute, $\frac{1}{2}$ of the material was placed in the Changed box to demonstrate the changing that occurs in radioactive materials. The passing of another minute results in placing $\frac{1}{2}$ of the remaining material in the Changed box, leaving only $\frac{1}{4}$ of the original material unchanged. At the end of 3 minutes, $\frac{1}{8}$ of the original material is left. The time it takes for half of a radioactive material to change is called its **half-life**. The half-life in this activity was thus 1 minute. It takes 10 to 12 minutes for the paper to become too small to cut. The paper pieces build up in the Changed box, but the pieces of paper in the Unchanged box get smaller as time passes. With enough time all radioactive materials will change, but for many of these materials it takes thousands of years for the change to occur.

We have created a simplified model to illustrate a complex topic—radioactivity.

Did You Know?

The half-life of plutonium-239, found in nuclear waste, is 24,000 years. At the end of 24,000 years, $^1/_2$ of all the stored radioactive plutonium-239 changes, but $^1/_2$ of the material remains unchanged. The used fuel rods from nuclear reactors containing plutonium-239 that are stored remain harmful for many thousands of years.

Solutions

1. a. *Think!*   How many children are skating?   3
How many children are present?   5
3 of the 5 children are skating.

Answer $^3/_5$ of the children are skating.

b. *Think!*   How many children are playing marbles?   2
How many children are present?   5
2 of the 5 children are playing marbles.

Answer $^2/_5$ of the children are playing marbles.

2. a. *Think!*   How many of the children are flying kites?   4
How many children are present?   7
4 of the 7 children are flying kites.

Answer $^4/_7$ of the children are flying kites.

b. *Think!*   How many of the children are sitting?   3
How many children are present?   7
3 of the 7 children are sitting.

Answer $^3/_7$ of the children are sitting.

2
Fractional Parts

Purpose To find the fractional parts.

Facts When determining the fractional part of a number follow
these steps:

Step 1 Write any whole numbers as fractions by placing the
number over 1.

Example

$$12 = \frac{12}{1}$$

Step 2 Multiply the numerators (the top numbers) and denominators (the bottom numbers) of the two fractions.

Examples

$$\frac{2}{3} \times \frac{12}{1} = \frac{2 \times 12}{3 \times 1} = \frac{24}{3}$$

$$\frac{3}{8} \times \frac{2}{4} = \frac{3 \times 2}{8 \times 4} = \frac{6}{32}$$

Step 3 Reduce the fraction to its simplest form.

Example When the numerator is larger than the denominator as in
²⁴/₃, the fraction can be reduced by dividing the numerator by the
denominator.

$$\begin{array}{r} 8 \\ 3\overline{)24} \\ \underline{24} \\ 0 \end{array}$$

If the denominator does not evenly divide into the numerator, as in the number 7/3, express the remainder as a fraction.

$$\begin{array}{r} 2 \\ 3\overline{)7} \\ \underline{6} \\ 1 \end{array}$$ ⟵ remainder

Answer   2 1/3

Example   When the numerator is smaller than the denominator, as in 6/32, divide the numerator and denominator by the largest **common factor**. A common factor is one number that will divide evenly into both the numerator and denominator.

$$\frac{6 \div 2}{32 \div 2} = \frac{3}{16}$$

Problems

Question 1   Carol spends 1/12 of each day studying. How many hours a day does this equal?

Think!   There are 24 hours in one day.

$$\frac{1}{12} \times 24 \text{ hours}$$

Step 1 $24 = \dfrac{24}{1}$

Step 2 $\dfrac{1}{12} \times \dfrac{24}{1} = \dfrac{1 \times 24}{12 \times 1} = \dfrac{24}{12}$

Step 3
$$\begin{array}{r} 2 \\ 12\overline{)24} \\ \underline{24} \\ 0 \end{array}$$

Answer   2 hours

Question 2 ¹/₂ of Mrs. Ruiz's science class are boys. ²/₃ of the boys in the class wear tennis shoes. What part or fraction of the class is made up of boys wearing tennis shoes?

Think! $\dfrac{1}{2} \times \dfrac{2}{3}$ = Number of boys wearing tennis shoes.

Step 1 $\dfrac{1 \times 2}{2 \times 3} = \dfrac{2}{6}$

Step 2 $\dfrac{2 \div 2}{6 \div 2} = \dfrac{1}{3}$

Answer ¹/₃ of the class consists of boys wearing tennis shoes.

Exercise

1. Patsy read 40 books during the month of August. Of these, ³/₄ were mystery books. How many mystery books did she read in August?

2. If ³/₅ of the 60 seeds planted by Wade grew, what was the total number of plants in his garden?

3. Amber spends ¹/₄ of each day sleeping. The amount of time that she sleeps during one year converts to how many days?

4. ³/₁₀ of the earth is land. North America makes up ¹/₆ of the land area. What part of the entire earth's surface is North America?

Activity: MIXTURE

Purpose   To demonstrate the fractional parts of air.

Materials   78 miniature   1 black gumdrop
                marshmallows   1 resealable plastic bag,
             21 red gumdrops   1 qt size

Procedure

■ Place the marshmallows and gumdrops in the plastic bag.

■ Close the bag and shake thoroughly to mix.

■ Dip your hand inside the plastic bag and scoop up some materials.

■ Count the number of marshmallows, red gumdrops, and black gumdrops in the sample taken from the bag.

Results   There will be fewer red gumdrops than there are marshmallows in any sample taken from the bag. The black gumdrop is rarely picked up.

Did You Know?

The mixture represents a sample of clean, dry air, which contains $^{78}/_{100}$ parts nitrogen (the marshmallows), $^{21}/_{100}$ parts oxygen (the red gumdrops), and $^{1}/_{100}$ part other gases (the black gumdrop). Samples of air taken from various places on the earth vary only slightly in composition.

Solutions

1. **Think!** $\frac{3}{4} \times 40 = ?$

   Step 1 $\frac{3 \times 40}{4 \times 1} = \frac{120}{4}$

   Step 2
   $$\begin{array}{r} 30 \\ 4\overline{)120} \\ \underline{12} \\ 000 \end{array}$$

   Answer   Patsy read 30 mystery books during August.

2. **Think!** $\frac{3}{5} \times 60 =$ Number of plants

   Step 1 $\frac{3 \times 60}{5 \times 1} = \frac{180}{5}$

Step 2

$$5\overline{)180} \\ \underline{15} \\ 30 \\ \underline{30} \\ 00$$

with quotient 36

Answer   36 plants

3.   **Think!**   1 year has 365 days

$$\frac{1}{4} \times 365 = \frac{1}{4} \times \frac{365}{1}$$

Step 1 $\dfrac{1 \times 365}{4 \times 1} = \dfrac{365}{4}$

Step 2

$$4\overline{)365} \\ \underline{36} \\ 005 \\ \underline{4} \\ 1 \quad \longleftarrow \text{ remainder}$$

with quotient 91

Answer   Amber sleeps enough hours each year to equal 91 1/4 days.

4.   **Think!** $\dfrac{3}{10} \times \dfrac{1}{6} = ?$

Step 1 $\dfrac{3 \times 1}{10 \times 6} = \dfrac{3}{60}$

Step 2 $\dfrac{3 \div 3}{60 \div 3} = \dfrac{1}{20}$

Answer   North America makes up 1/20 of the entire earth's surface.

3
Equivalents

Purpose   To write equivalent fractions.

Facts   Equivalent fractions represent the same amount of a whole or group. $1/2$ of a circle is the same amount as $2/4$ of the same circle. This is expressed as: $1/2 = 2/4$. It is just as true to say that $2/4 = 1/2$. When changing a fraction with a small denominator to one with a larger denominator, multiply the numerator and denominator by the same number. To change a fraction with a large denominator to one with a smaller denominator, divide the numerator and denominator by the same number.

Problems

Question 1   Make the fractions equivalent.

$$\frac{1}{2} = \frac{?}{4}$$

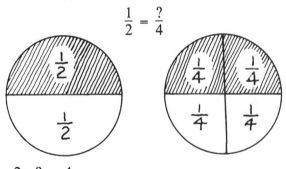

Think! $2 \times ? = 4$

$$\frac{1 \times 2}{2 \times 2} = \frac{2}{4}$$

Answer $\dfrac{1}{2} = \dfrac{2}{4}$

Question 2 Make the fractions equivalent.

$$\frac{6}{8} = \frac{?}{4}$$

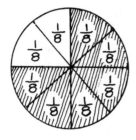 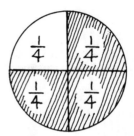

Think! $\qquad 8 \div ? = 4$

$$\frac{6 \div 2}{8 \div 2} = \frac{3}{4}$$

Answer $\qquad \frac{6}{8} = \frac{3}{4}$

Exercises

1. Sterling ate 4/8 of a doughnut. Beulah's donut is cut into four parts. How many parts must Beulah eat to equal what Sterling ate?

$$\frac{4}{8} = \frac{?}{4}$$

2. Tina cut a birthday cake into 16 equal pieces. Each person ate 1 piece of cake. How many people were served if ³/₄ of the cake was eaten?

$$\frac{3}{4} = \frac{?}{16}$$

*3. Lauren uses 100 coins to teach fractions to her sister Lacey. Determine how many pennies each fractional part of 100 represents.

a. $\frac{3}{4}$ of 100

b. $\frac{4}{25}$ of 100

Activity: ONE LESS

Purpose   To demonstrate that equivalent fractions represent the same amount.

Materials   1 sheet of lined notebook   ruler
                       paper   scissors
                   pencil

Procedure

■ Lay the ruler along the top line of the paper.

■ Start at the left margin and make a 6-in. (15-cm) mark over the line on the lined notebook paper.

- Move to the next line and make another 6-in. (15-cm) mark.

- Repeat until 7 separate marks are made.

- Place the ruler diagonally across the lines so that the ruler's edge touches the left end of the top line and the right end of the bottom line.

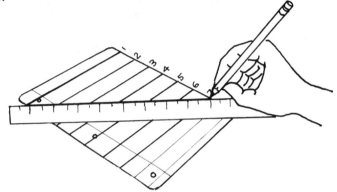

- Draw along the edge of the ruler, extending the lines to the edges of the paper.

- Use the scissors to cut across the diagonal line.

- Keep the paper pieces flat on a table and slide the right piece down to form 6 straight lines.

- Measure the length of each line.

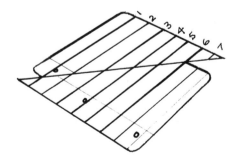

Results   Each of the 7 lines is 6 in. (15 cm) long. Shifting the paper pieces causes one of the lines to disappear and produces 6 lines that are each 7 in. (17.5 cm) long. The sum of the length of the 7 lines is 42 in. (105 cm), which is equivalent to the sum of the length of the 6

lines. The 6 separate parts are equivalent to the 7 separate parts and can be expressed in fraction form as $^6/_6 = ^7/_7$.

Did You Know?

You spend about $^1/_4$ of your life sleeping. This is equal to 2,190 hours each year. To determine how many hours you have slept thus far in your life, multiply your age by 2,190. There are 8,760 hours in a year. What fraction of that time do you spend studying math?

Solutions

1. *Think!*

$$8 \div ? = 4$$

$$\frac{4 \div 2}{8 \div 2} = \frac{2}{4}$$

$$\frac{4}{8} = \frac{2}{4}$$

Answer Beulah must eat 2 parts.

2. *Think!*

$$4 \times ? = 16$$

$$\frac{3 \times 4}{4 \times 4} = \frac{12}{16}$$

$$\frac{3}{4} = \frac{12}{16}$$

Answer 12 people were served.

3. a. *Think!*

$$4 \times ? = 100$$

$$\frac{3 \times 25}{4 \times 25} = \frac{75}{100}$$

$$\frac{3}{4} = \frac{75}{100}$$

Answer 75 pennies

3. b. *Think* $25 \times ? = 100$

$$\frac{4 \times 4}{25 \times 4} = \frac{16}{100}$$

$$\frac{4}{25} = \frac{16}{100}$$

Answer   16 pennies

4
Averages

Purpose To calculate averages.

Facts Averages give general information about collected facts. Average rainfall for a year does not tell the rainfall on any specific day, but it does provide the information to compare rainfall from year to year. Because rain collects in lakes and reservoirs, the year-to-year comparison can indicate the area's dryness.

Grades recorded on school reports are an average of scores in each subject during a specific number of days. Lauren's math grades during the grading period were 86, 97, 94, 89, 95, and 91. To determine her math grade average, follow these steps:

Step 1 Find the sum of the scores:

$$86 + 97 + 94 + 89 + 95 + 91 = 552$$

Step 2 Divide the sum by the total number of scores, 6:

$$
\begin{array}{r}
92 \quad \longleftarrow \text{Average} \\
6\overline{)552} \quad \longleftarrow \text{Sum of scores} \\
\underline{54} \\
12 \\
\underline{12} \\
0
\end{array}
$$

Number of scores $\longrightarrow$

Problem

Question Davin's bowling scores are 125, 135, 150, and 134. Determine his average score.

Step 1 Find the sum of the scores:

$$125 + 135 + 150 + 134 = 544$$

Step 2 Divide the sum of the scores by the total number of scores, 4:

$$
\begin{array}{r}
136 \\
4\overline{)544} \\
\end{array}
$$

Number of scores ———→ 4)544 ←——— Sum of scores

136 ←——— Average score

$$
\begin{array}{r}
136 \\
4\,\overline{)\,544\,} \\
4 \\
\hline
14 \\
12 \\
\hline
24 \\
24 \\
\hline
0
\end{array}
$$

Answer   136

Exercises

1. Determine the average number of students present in Mrs. Duham's sewing classes during the week of August 1 through August 7.

Attendance Sheet

August 1990	Number of Students
1	95
2	96
3	100
4	101
5	102
6	97
7	95

2. A gymnast receives scores in different gymnastic events. Determine her average score.

Jennifer Lynn

Gymnastic Event	Score
Floor exercise	9.8
Parallel bars	9.2
Uneven bars	9.9
Vault	9.7
Balancing beam	10.0

3. Matthew counted his food calories for 1 week. What was his average daily calorie intake for the week?

Matthew

Day	Calorie Intake
Monday	1200
Tuesday	1300
Wednesday	1500
Thursday	1200
Friday	1800
Saturday	2200
Sunday	2000

*4. The average age of Stella Cathey's children is 22 years. What is Carol's age?

Age of Stella's Children

Children	Age (Years)
Jim	23
Frances	24
Carol	?
Group Average	22

Activity: HOW LONG?

Purpose   To determine the average length of a peanut.

Material   20 peanuts in the shell
ruler

Procedure

■ Measure and record the length of each peanut to the nearest inch (centimeter).

■ Add the 20 length measurements.

■ Divide the sum of the length measurements by the number of peanuts, 20.

Results   The sum of the lengths divided by the total number of peanuts measured gives the average length of the peanuts measured. Peanuts generally range from 1 to 2 in. (2½ to 5 cm) in length.

Did You Know?

There are about 250 average-sized peanuts in 1 pound (454 g) of peanuts. Peanuts are one of the most nutritious of all vegetables. There is more protein in a pound of peanuts than in a pound of meat.

Solutions

1. Step 1   Find the sum of the students:

$$95 + 96 + 100 + 101 + 102 + 97 + 95 = 686$$

Step 2   Divide the sum of the students by the total number of days, 7:

$$
\begin{array}{r}
98 \quad \longleftarrow \quad \text{Average attendance} \\
\text{Number of days} \longrightarrow \quad 7\overline{)686} \quad \longleftarrow \quad \text{Sum of students} \\
\underline{63} \\
56 \\
\underline{56} \\
0
\end{array}
$$

Answer 98 is the average attendance.

2. Step 1   Find the sum of the scores:

$$9.8 + 9.2 + 9.9 + 9.7 + 10.0 = 48.6$$

Step 2   Divide the sum by the total number of scores, 5:

$$
\begin{array}{r}
9.72 \quad \longleftarrow \quad \text{Average} \\
\text{Number of scores} \longrightarrow \quad 5\overline{)48.60} \quad \longleftarrow \quad \text{Sum of scores} \\
\underline{45} \\
36 \\
\underline{35} \\
10 \\
\underline{10} \\
0
\end{array}
$$

Answer   9.72

3. Step 1   Find the sum of the calories:

$$1200 + 1300 + 1500 + 1200 + 1800 + 2200 + 2000 = 11,200$$

Step 2   Divide the sum of the calories by the number of days, 7:

$$
\begin{array}{r}
1600 \quad \longleftarrow \quad \text{Average} \\
\text{Number of days} \longrightarrow \quad 7\overline{)11200} \quad \longleftarrow \quad \text{Sum of calories} \\
\underline{7} \\
42 \\
\underline{42} \\
0
\end{array}
$$

Answer 1600 calories

*4. *Think!* $3 \times 22 = 66$

    Think!   You now know that the sum of the three ages is:
$23 + 24 + ? = 66$

    Think!   The sum of $23 + 24 = 47$, therefore:
$47 + ? = 66$

    Answer $? = 19$
Carol is 19 years old.

5

Multiples

Purpose   To multiply whole and decimal numbers.

Facts   The numbers that are multiplied together are called **factors** and the answer of the multiplication is the **product**. Multiply factors with decimals as you would whole numbers, placing the decimal in the product. The number of decimal places in the product is equal to the sum of the decimal places in all of the factors.

Example

Factor		Factor		Product
2.2	×	1.81	=	3.982
1 place	+	2 places	=	3 places

When multiplying three or more factors, multiply the first two numbers and then multiply the product by the next factor. Continue this until all the factors are used.

Example $4 \times 3 \times 2 \times 5 =$
$4 \times 3 = 12$
$12 \times 2 = 24$
$24 \times 5 = 120$
or
$4 \times 3 \times 2 \times 5 = 120$

When the factors have more than one number, work with one number at a time.

Example

3.2	1 decimal place
× 4.5	1 decimal place
160	Product of 3.2×5
+ 128	Product of 3.2×4
14.40	2 decimal places

Problem

Question   Multiply 1.23 × 0.81 × 4

Think!   Multiply the first two factors:

1.23	2 decimal places
× 0.81	2 decimal places
123	Product of 1.23 × 1
984	Product of 1.23 × 8
9963	

Think!   Multiply the product, 9963, by 4:

9963	
× 4	
39852	

Think!   What is the sum of the decimal places in the three factors?   4

Answer   3.9852

Exercises

1. Charlotte can run one lap around the school track in 1.45 minutes. To determine how long it would take her to run 1.5 laps, multiply 1.45 × 1.5.

2. Lacey ate 2.5 cookies. Every cookie contained 4.5 raisins. To determine the total number of raisins eaten by Lacey, multiply 2.5 × 4.5.

3. Diane wants to cover her biology folder with stickers of trees. She needs 2.25 stickers to cover the width and 3.5 stickers to cover the length. To determine the number of stickers needed to cover the front and back of the notebook, multiply 2.25 × 3.5 × 2.

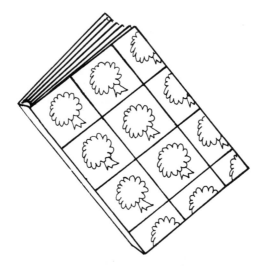

*4. Would you take this job? A job pays $.01 the first day. If the pay doubles each day, the money received on day two would be twice the pay received on the previous day, or 2 × $.01 = $.02. Calculate the money received each day for 30 days starting with day 1 = $.01.

Activity: **DOUBLING**

Purpose To determine the number of sections formed by folding a sheet of paper a specific number of times.

Materials typing paper
newspaper

Procedure

- Fold the typing paper in half to produce 2 sections.

- Fold the paper in half again to produce 4 sections.

- Continue to fold the paper until 6 folds have been made.

- Determine the number of sections produced by doubling the section number after each folding.

■ Open the paper after the sixth folding and count the sections to check your calculated answer.

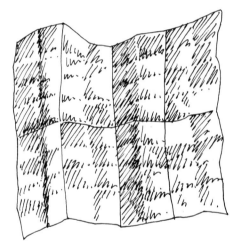

■ Refold the typing paper and determine how many times it can be folded in half.

■ Use the newspaper sheet and determine how many times it can be folded in half.

Results   Six folds produce 64 sections. It is difficult to fold any size paper more than six times because of the thickness of the paper. The seventh fold produces 128 sections and an eighth fold would again double the number of sections, forming 256 sections.

Solutions

1.   1.45 ⟵——— 2 decimal places
    × 1.5 ⟵——— 1 decimal place
    ——————
    725
    145
    ——————
    2.175 ⟵——— 3 decimal places

Answer   2.175 minutes to run 1.5 laps

2.   2.5 ⟵——— 1 decimal place
    × 4.5 ⟵——— 1 decimal place
    ——————
    125
    100
    ——————
    11.25 ⟵——— 2 decimal places

Answer 11.25 raisins (*Note:* This is the same as 11 1/4.)

3.   2.25 ⟵——— 2 decimal places
    × 3.5 ⟵——— 1 decimal place
    ——————
    1125
    675
    ——————
    7875
    × 2
    ——————
    15.750 ⟵——— 3 decimal places

Answer   15.750 stickers (*Note:* This is the same as 15 3/4.)

*4.

Day	Salary ($)	Day	Salary ($)
1	.01	10	5.12
2	.02	11	10.24
3	.04	12	20.48
4	.08	13	40.96
5	.16	14	81.92
6	.32	15	163.84
7	.64	16	327.68
8	1.28	17	655.36
9	2.56	18	1310.72

Day	Salary ($)	Day	Salary ($)
19	2621.44	25	167,772.16
20	5242.88	26	335,544.32
21	10,485.76	27	671,088.64
22	20,971.52	28	1,342,177.28
23	41,943.04	29	2,684,354.56
24	83,886.08	30	5,368,709.12

Note that each day's salary was twice as much as the day before. A total amount of money received for any number of days can be quickly calculated by doubling the pay for the last day of work, then subtract day 1 from the product. Example: How much money was received during 4 days?

$$\text{Salary for day 4} = \$.08$$
$$\frac{\times\ 2}{\$.16}$$

$$\text{Product} - .01 = \text{Total money received}$$
$$\$.16 - .01 = \$.15 = \text{Total money for 4 days}$$

To check your answer, add up the money received during the four days.

$$\$.01 + \$.02 + \$.04 + \$.08 + \ = \$.15$$

The total amount of money received during the 30 days:

$$\$5,368,709.12 \times 2 = \$10,737,418.24$$
$$\$10,737,418.24 - .01 = \$10,737,418.23$$

II
Measurements

6
Centimeters

Purpose To use a metric ruler to measure lengths in centimeter units.

Facts On a metric ruler, the printed numbers indicate centimeter measurements. Each small division between the numbers is equal to 0.1 cm.

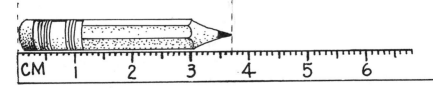

Problem

Question Determine the length of the pencil in centimeters. Express the answer to the nearest 0.1 cm.

Answer The length of the pencil is 3.7 cm.

Exercises

1. What is the length of the adhesive bandage?

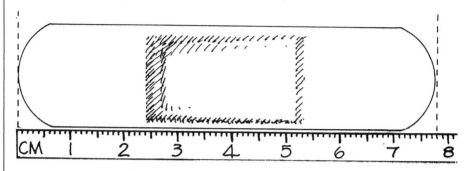

2. How long is the paper clip?

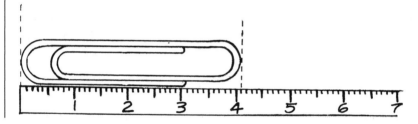

Activity: SPAN

Purpose   To measure lengths in spans and centimeters.

Materials   hand   masking tape
                  metric ruler   pencil
                  table (the kitchen table will work well)

Procedure

- Stretch out the fingers on your left hand.

- Lay your stretched hand on top of the ruler, placing your little finger on the end of the ruler and stretching your thumb as far up the ruler as it will go.

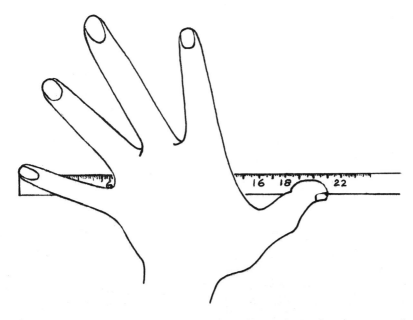

- Record the length of your stretched hand to the nearest whole centimeter.

- Place a strip of tape along the longest edge of the table.

- Lay your stretched hand at the left end of the table edge on top of the tape.

- Mark the end of your thumb with the pencil.

- Move your stretched hand to the right, placing the end of your little finger on the pencil mark.

- Again mark the end of your thumb.

- Continue to move your hand across the edge of the table until the entire length of the table has been measured.

- If the last measurement is shorter than your stretched hand, count it only if the distance is more than half the distance across your stretched hand.

- Your stretched hand is called a **span.** Count the number of marks made and record the length of the table in spans.

- Multiply the number of spans times the centimeter length of your stretched hand to determine the length of the table in centimeters.

Results   The number of marks will depend on the length of the table and how long the span of your hand is. If you remember the length of your hand span, it will give you a handy way to estimate lengths.

Did You Know?

Our measuring system was originally based on human measurements such as the span of your hand. A mile was equal to 1,000 steps of a Roman soldier and a yard was the length from the king's nose to the end of his thumb. Since the king was not always available, each person used his or her own outstretched arm to measure a yard.

The differences in the sizes of human bodies led to the need for a more standard way of measuring. In 1791, French scientists created the metric system of measurements. One ten-millionth of the distance from the North Pole to the Equator was scratched on a metal rod. Copies of the metal rod were made and used to measure metric lengths. With technological advancements, more precise measurements are possible. The distance that light travels in 1/299,792,458 of a second is now the standard meter length.

Solutions

1. The length of the adhesive bandage is 7.8 cm.

2. The length of the paper clip is 4.1 cm.

7
Millimeters

Purpose   To use a metric ruler to measure length in millimeter units.

Facts   On a metric ruler, the printed numbers indicate centimeter measurements. Each small division between the numbers is equal to 0.1 centimeters, which is the same as 1 millimeter. One centimeter equals 10 millimeters. Multiply each numbered centimeter measurement by 10. The symbol for the millimeter unit is mm.

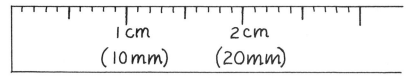

1 cm   2 cm
(10 mm)   (20 mm)

Problem

Question   What is the width of the ribbon in millimeter (mm) units?

Answer   The printed numbers on the ruler times 10 give a millimeter measurement. Each small division between the printed numbers equals 1 millimeter measurement. The edge of the ribbon stops at the second millimeter mark after the printed number 2 on the ruler. The width of the ribbon is equal to 22 mm.

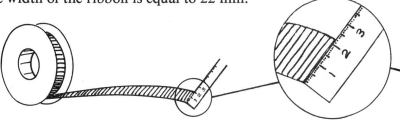

Exercises

1. What is the length of the comb in millimeters?

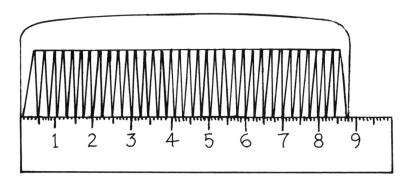

2. How tall are the bristles on the toothbrush in millimeters?

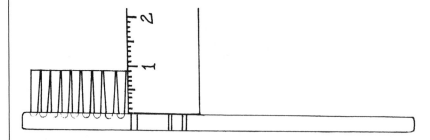

*3. There are 100 pages in the book. What is the thickness in millimeters of each page?

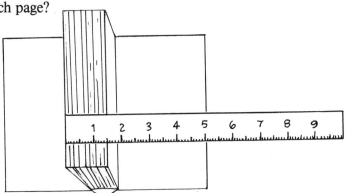

Activity: METRIC TAPE

Purpose   To make and measure millimeter lengths with a paper metric tape.

Materials   typing paper   marking pen
                 scissors   large chicken egg

Procedure

- Measure and cut a 30 mm × 280 mm paper strip.

- Use the pencil to write ZERO across one end of the paper strip.

- Lay the ruler on the paper strip and use the pencil to mark the millimeter positions on the paper. Begin on the very edge of the paper strip marked ZERO.

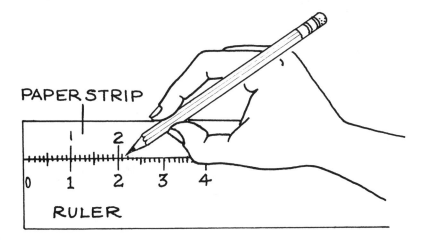

- Use the paper measuring tape you just made to measure a large chicken egg from end to end.

Results   The paper tape easily bends around objects, making it useful when measuring curved materials. The length of a chicken egg from end to end varies with each egg. The author's large egg measured 83 mm from end to end. Measure different-sized eggs and compare their measurements.

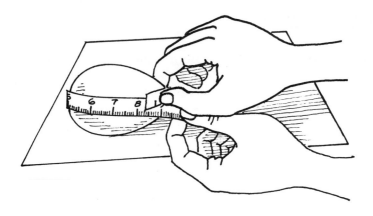

Did You Know?

The smallest bird egg is laid by the Vervain hummingbird of Jamaica. The egg measures about 9.9 mm in length (from end to end.

Solutions

1. The comb is 88 mm long.

2. The toothbrush bristles are 9 mm long.

*3. The thickness of 100 pages is 15 mm. To determine the width of one page, divide 15 mm by 100.

$$
\begin{array}{r}
.15 \\
100\overline{)15.00} \\
\underline{10\ 0} \\
5\ 00 \\
\underline{5\ 00} \\
0\ 00
\end{array}
$$

The thickness of one page is 0.15 mm.

8
Perimeter

Purpose   To find the perimeter of polygons.

Facts   The **perimeter** is the distance around an object and can be found by adding the lengths of all sides. **Polygons** have straight sides that meet to form angles.

Problems

Question   Determine the perimeter of each object.

1. **a.** The perimeter of the rectangular picture frame can be determined by adding together the length of all four sides:

English
10 in. + 12 in. + 10 in. + 12 in. = 44 in.

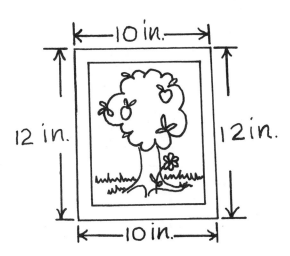

Metric

25 cm + 30 cm + 25 cm + 30 cm = 110 cm

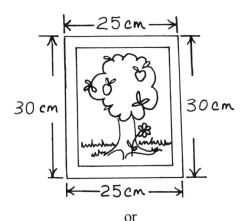

or

Determine the distance halfway around the rectangle and multiply by two:

English

Step 1   10 in. + 12 in. = 22 in.
Step 2   22 in. × 2 = 44 in.

Metric

Step 1   25 cm + 30 cm = 55 cm
Step 2   55 cm × 2 = 110 cm

2. b. The perimeter of the square table top can be determined by adding together the length of all four sides:

English

1.5 yd + 1.5 yd + 1.5 yd + 1.5 yd = 6.0 yd

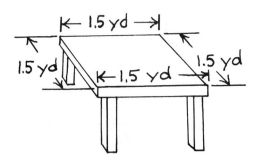

Metric
1.37 m + 1.37 m + 1.37 m + 1.37 m = 5.48 m

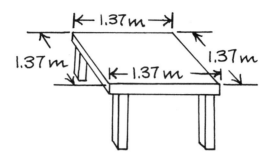

Since all four sides are the same length, multiply the measurement of one of the sides by four:

English

1.5 yd × 4 = 6.0 yd

Metric

1.37 m × 4 = 5.48 m

3. c. The perimeter of this irregularly shaped park can be determined by adding all the sides together:

English
3 mi + 2 mi + 4 mi + 5 mi + 4 = 18 mi

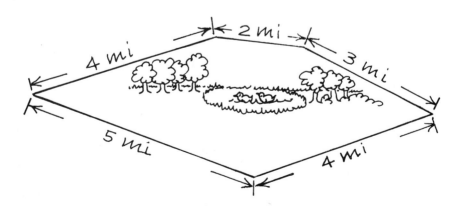

Metric
4.8 km + 3.2 km + 6.4 km + 8 km + 6.4 km = 28.8 km

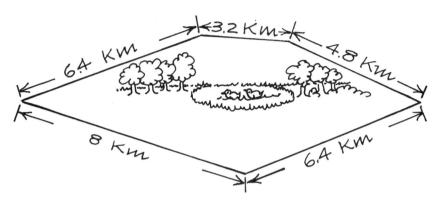

Exercises

1. A rectangle has measurements of 100 in. (254 cm) × 59 in. (150 cm). What is the perimeter of the structure?

2. Determine the perimeter of this irregularly shaped polygon.

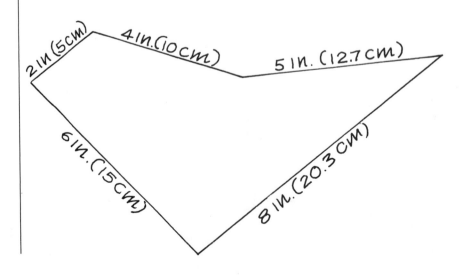

*3. Arrange the four squares to form a structure with a perimeter of:
  (a)   16 in. (40 cm)
  (b)   20 in. (50 cm)
  (c)   24 in. (60 cm)

   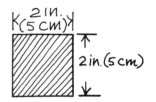

Activity: ROLLER

Purpose   To construct and use a measuring wheel.

Materials   scissors   ruler
              index card   book
              pencil   coffee can lid
              marking pen

Procedure   Use these instructions to make a measuring wheel.

■ Cut a ½ in. × 1 in. (1 cm × 3 cm) strip from the index card.

■ Mark a line in the center of the shorter sides of the paper strip to indicate ¼ in. (½ cm) length.

■ Use the marking pen to draw a 2 in. (5 cm) line from the lid's edge toward the center of the lid.

■ With the marking pen, write the word BEGIN on the 2 in. (5 cm) line on the lid.

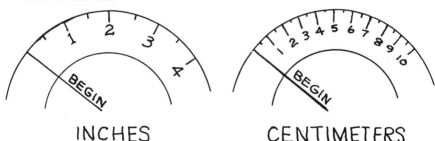

INCHES   CENTIMETERS

■ Use the paper strip to indicate the position of ¼ in. (½ cm) sections around the edge of the lid. Start with the BEGIN line and mark each ¼ in. (½ cm) section with the marking pen.

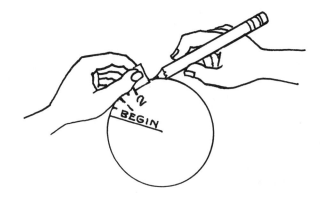

■ To measure inches, number every fourth line. (Number every second line to measure centimeters.)

■ Insert one-half the length of the pencil through the center of the plastic lid.

■ Place the BEGIN line on the edge of a book.

■ Measure the perimeter of the book by holding the pencil and rolling the lid around the outer edge of the book.

Results   The perimeter of the book is determined by the number of turns of the lid plus any fraction of a turn.

Did You Know?

Trundle wheels similar to your measuring wheel are used to measure distances. The perimeter of houses or distances between the bases on a baseball field can be quickly measured with a trundle wheel that measures one meter with each turn.

Solutions

1. The perimeter of the rectangular shape can be determined by adding the length of all four sides together:

100 in. + 59 in. + 100 in. + 59 in. = 318 in.
(254 cm + 150 cm + 254 cm + 150 cm = 808 cm)

or

by determining the distance halfway around the rectangle and multiplying by two:

English
Step 1   100 in. + 59 in. = 159 in.
Step 2   159 in. × 2 = 318 in.

Metric
Step 1   254 cm + 150 cm = 404 cm
Step 2   404 cm × 2 = 808 cm

2. The perimeter of irregularly shaped polygons can be determined by adding the length of all the sides together.

English
2 in. + 4 in. + 5 in. + 8 in. + 6 in. = 25 in.

Metric
5 cm + 10 cm + 12.7 cm + 20.3 cm + 15 cm = 63 cm

*3 **a.** Arrange the four squares to form one large square.

    Think!   Number of sides × Length of each side = Perimeter
             8 sides × 2 in. (5 cm) = 16 in. (40 cm)

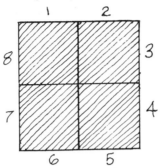

b. Place the squares side by side to form a straight line.

    Think!   Number of sides × Length of each side = Perimeter
             10 sides × 2 in. (5 cm) = 20 in. (50 cm)

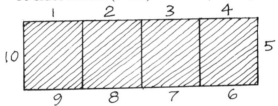

c. Arrange the squares to form a cross shape.

    Think!   Number of sides × Length of each side = Perimeter
             12 sides × 2 in. (5 cm) = 24 in. (60 cm)

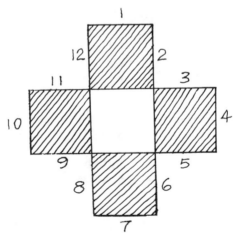

9
Diameter of a Circle

Purpose   To measure the diameter of a circle.

Facts   A straight line that begins and ends on a circle is called a **chord**. A chord that passes through the center of a circle is called a **diameter**. Any line that connects the center of a circle to any point on the circle's edge is called a **radius**. A radius is equal to one-half the length of the diameter.

Problems

Question   Study the diagrams and determine either the length of the radius or the diameter of each.

English

a. Diameter = 8 in.
    Radius = ¹/₂ of the diameter
           = ¹/₂ × 8 in.
           = 4 in.

Metric

    Diameter = 20 cm
    Radius = ¹/₂ of the diameter
           = ¹/₂ × 20 cm
           = 10 cm

English

b. Radius $= 2$ in.
   Diameter $= 2 \times$ radius
   $= 2 \times 2$ in.
   $= 4$ in.

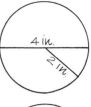

Metric

   Radius $= 5$ cm
   Diameter $= 2 \times$ radius
   $= 2 \times 5$ cm
   $= 10$ cm

Exercises

1. Study the diagrams and determine the length of the radius and the diameter of each.

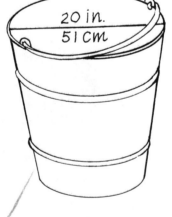

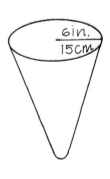

*2. Three chords are used in the diagram to cut the circle into 7 parts. Use 5 chords to cut a circle into 16 parts.

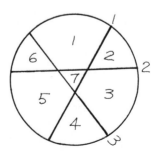

Activity: CENTER POINT

Purpose   To find the center of a circle.

Materials   index card   typing paper
               pencil   drinking glass
               paper   ruler

Procedure

■ Place the glass upside down on the paper.

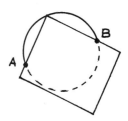

■ Use the pencil to draw a circle by marking around the outside of the glass.

■ Remove the glass from the paper.

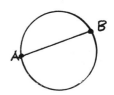

■ Place a corner of the index card so that it touches any point on the edge of the circle, then mark points A and B on the circle as in the diagram.

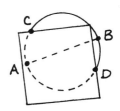

■ Use the ruler to draw a line between points A and B.

■ Place the corner of the card so that it touches a different place on the circle's edge, and mark points C and D as in the diagram.

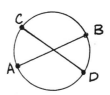

■ Use the ruler to draw a line between points C and D.

Results The lines intersect in the center of the circle. It will not matter where you place the card or how many lines you draw, they will all intersect in the center of the circle.

Did You Know?

The average diameter of a human hair is about 0.0635 mm.

Solutions

1. a. English
　　Radius　　= 4 in.
　　Diameter = 2 × radius
　　　　　　= 2 × 4 in.
　　　　　　= 8 in.

　　Metric
　　Radius　　= 10 cm
　　Diameter = 2 × radius
　　　　　　= 2 × 10 cm
　　　　　　= 20 cm

b. English
　　Diameter = 20 in.
　　Radius　　= ½ of diameter
　　　　　　= ½ × 20 in.
　　　　　　= 10 in.

　　Metric
　　Diameter = 51 cm
　　Radius　　= ½ diameter
　　　　　　= ½ × 51 cm
　　　　　　= 25.5 cm

c. English
　　Radius　　= 6 in.
　　Diameter = 2 × radius
　　　　　　= 2 × 6 in.
　　　　　　= 12 in.

Metric
Radius   = 15 cm
Diameter = 2 × radius
         = 2 × 15 cm
         = 30 cm

*2.

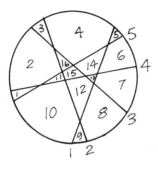 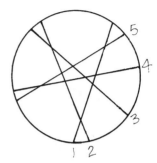

10
Circumference of a Circle

Purpose To determine the circumference of a circle using the formula $c = \pi \times d$.

Facts The formula $c = \pi \times d$ is read as:

Circumference = pi times Diameter

The **circumference** of any circle divided by its diameter equals approximately 3.14. This number, 3.14, is called pi (symbolized by π, a Greek letter) and is the same for all circles regardless of their size.

Note: You have just learned one of the really neat things about math. There are *relationships* that, once discovered, hold true everywhere and for everyone in the universe! No matter how big the circle is or what it is made of or who makes it, pi is *always* 3.14.

Problem

Question Determine the circumference of each circle using the formula.

1. a.

English

$$\text{Diameter} = 4 \text{ in.}$$
$$\pi = 3.14$$
Formula: $c = \pi \times d$
$$= 3.14 \times 4 \text{ in.}$$
$$= 12.56 \text{ in.}$$

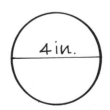

4 in.

Metric

Diameter = 10 cm
π = 3.14
Formula: c = π × d
         = 3.14 × 10 cm
         = 31.4 cm

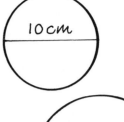

1. b.

English

Radius = 3 in.
Diameter = 2 × 3 in. = 6 in.
π = 3.14
Formula: c = π × d
         = 3.14 × 6 in.
         = 18.84 in.

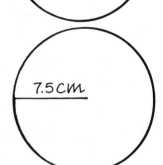

Metric

Radius = 7.5 cm
Diameter = 2 × 7.5 cm = 15 cm
π = 3.14
Formula: c = π × d
         = 3.14 × 15 cm
         = 47.1 cm

Exercises

1. Determine the circumference of a circle with

a. A diameter of 10 in. (25 cm)

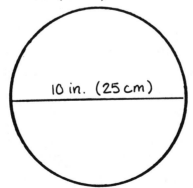

b. A radius of 6 in. (15 cm)

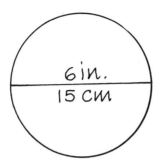

2. A child is swinging an 80-in. (200-cm) long rope. How far does the ball attached to the end of the rope travel in one complete turn?

3. A phonograph record has a radius of 5.5 in. (14 cm). How far does a point on the edge of the record travel in four turns?

Activity: RUN AROUND

Purpose   To draw circles of different diameters.

Materials   2 pencils   scissors
                 string   ruler
                 paper

Procedure

■ Cut a piece of string about 6 in. (15 cm) long.

■ Tie one end of the string around a pencil and tie a loop in the other end of the string.

■ Place the loop in the center of the paper.

■ Stand a second pencil in the center of the loop with the eraser touching the paper and hold this pencil stationary.

■ Pull the pencil tied to the string outward to stretch the string.

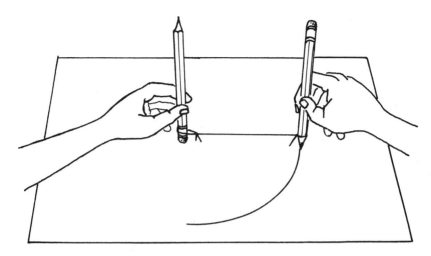

■ Move the tied pencil around with its point pressed against the paper until a complete circle is drawn.

■ Change the length of the string and repeat.

Results   The point of the pencil marks the outline of a circle. The length of the string is equal to the **radius** of the circle. As the length of the string—the radius—increases, the size of the circle increases.

Did You Know?

The circumference of the earth at the equator is 24,901.46 miles (39,842.336 km). The circumference around the earth's poles is 45 miles (72 km) less than around the equator.

Solutions

1. a.

> **English**
> Diameter = 10 in.
> π = 3.14
> Formula: c = $\pi \times$ d
>   = 3.14 × 10 in.
>   = 31.4 in.

Metric
Diameter = 25 cm
π = 3.14
Formula: c = $\pi \times$ d
= 3.14 $\times$ 25
= 78.5 cm

1. b.

English
Radius = 6 in.
Diameter = 2 $\times$ 6 in. = 12 in.
π = 3.14
Formula: c = $\pi \times$ d
= 3.14 $\times$ 12 in.
= 37.68 in.

Metric
Radius = 15 cm
Diameter = 2 $\times$ 15 cm = 30 cm
π = 3.14
Formula: c = $\pi \times$ d
= 3.14 $\times$ 30 cm
= 94.2 cm

2. The length of the rope equals the radius of the circle, and the distance traveled by the ball in one turn equals the circumference of the circle.

English
Radius = 80 in.
Diameter = 2 $\times$ 80 in. = 160 in.
π = 3.14
Formula: c = $\pi \times$ d
= 3.14 $\times$ 160 in.
= 502.4 in.

Metric
Radius = 200 cm
Diameter = 2×200 cm = 400 cm
π = 3.14
Formula: c = $\pi \times d$
= 3.14×400 cm
= 1256 cm

3. The distance traveled by a point on the edge of the record in four turns is equal to four times the circumference of the record.

English
Radius = 5.5 in.
Diameter = 2×5.5 in. = 11 in.
π = 3.14
Formula: c = $\pi \times d$
= 3.14×11 in.
= 34.54 in.
Total distance = $4 \times c$
= 4×34.54 in.
= 138.16 in.

Metric
Radius = 14 cm
Diameter = 2×14 cm = 28 cm
π = 3.14
Formula: c = $\pi \times d$
= 3.14×28 cm
= 87.92 cm
Total distance = $4 \times c$
= 4×87.92 cm
= 351.68 cm

11
Area of Rectangles and Squares

Purpose To find the area of a rectangle or square using the formula $A = L \times W$.

Facts The formula $A = L \times W$ is read as:

Area = Length times Width

Sides a and b of the diagram may be labeled as either the length or the width without changing the result.

Example 1
English
A = Length × Width
  = 4 in. × 2 in.
  = 8 in.^{2}

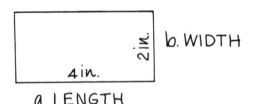

Metric
A = Length × Width
  = 10 cm × 5 cm
  = 50 cm^2

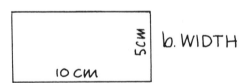

Example 2
English
A = Length × Width
  = 2 in × 4 in.
  = 8 in.^{2}

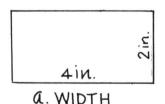

Metric

A = Length × Width
  = 10 cm × 5 cm
  = 50 cm^2

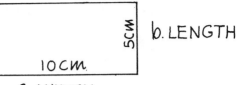

a. WIDTH

b. LENGTH

When two units are multiplied, such as ft × ft, a small 2 is placed to the upper right of the unit, ft^2, and the combination is read as square feet. (m^2 is read as square meters.)

Problem

Question   If the president's desk in the Oval Office is 5.5 ft (1.7 m) long and 4 ft (1.2 m) wide, what is the desk's surface area?

English

A = Length × Width
  = 4 ft × 5.5 ft
  = 22 ft^2

Metric

A = Length × Width
  = 1.2 m × 1.7 m
  = 2.04 m^2

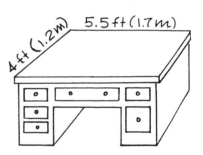

Exercises

1. What is the area of the bulletin board?

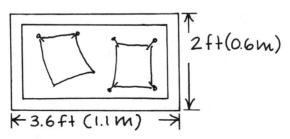

2. Colorado is nearly rectangular. Determine its area.

*3. One quart (liter) of paint will cover an area of 110 ft² (10.2 m²). Is one quart (liter) enough paint to cover a wall 13 ft (4 m) wide and 8 ft (2.4 m) high?

Activity: **BIGGER**

Purpose To determine how area affects the speed of falling objects.

Materials
plastic garbage bag	scissors
string	ruler
2 small washers of equal size and weight	

Procedure

- Cut eight strings, each about 24 in. (60 cm) long.

- Measure and cut a 10 in. (25 cm) square from the plastic bag.

- Tie a string to each corner of the plastic sheet (parachute).

- Be sure the four free strings are the same length, then tie all four ends together in a knot.

- Use a string about 6 in. (15 cm) long to attach a washer to the knot joining the parachute strings.

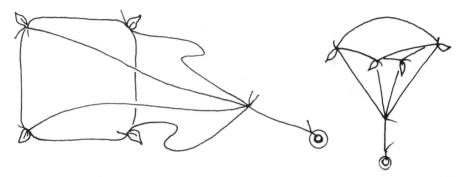

- Make a second larger parachute using a 24 in. (60 cm) square of plastic and the four remaining strings.

- Tie the four strings in a knot and attach the washer to the knot with a 6 in. (15 cm) string as before.

- To test the parachutes, hold each in the center of the plastic sheet. Flatten the plastic.

- Fold the plastic in half.

- Loosely wrap the string around the folded plastic.

- Throw the parachutes up into the air, one at a time, and observe the time it takes for each to reach the ground.

Results   The larger parachute opens and floats to the ground more slowly than does the smaller parachute. The washers are the same weight, with the same air resistance, and do not affect the relative speed.

Did You Know?

Objects hit against air as they fall. The larger the surface of a falling object, the more air it collects as it falls. Gravity pulls things down, but the collected air under the falling object pushes upward. A parachute with its collected air slows the fall of a person. Some insects have such a large surface area as compared to their weight that they can fall from a tall building and walk away unharmed.

Solutions

1.

English

A = Length × Width
  = 3.6 ft^2 × 2 ft
  = 7.2 ft^2

Metric

A = Length × Width
  = 1.1 m × .6 m
  = .66 m^2

2.

English

A = Length × Width
  = 368 mi × 285 mi
  = 104,880 mi^2

Metric

A = Length × Width
A = 589 km × 456 km
  = 268,584 km^2

*3.

English

A = Length × Width
  = 13 ft × 8 ft
  = 104 ft^2

Think!   110 ft^2 is covered by 1 quart. 104 ft^2 is less than 110 ft^2.

Answer Yes, 1 quart is enough paint.

Metric

A = Length × Width

    = 4 m × 2.4 m

    = 9.6 m^2

Think!   10.2 m^2 is covered by 1 quart. 9.6 m^2 is less than 10.2 m^2.

Answer Yes, 1 liter is enough paint.

12
Area of Triangles

Purpose   To find the area of a triangle using the formula A = ¹/₂ × b × h.

Facts   **Triangle:** a plane with three sides that meet to form three vertices or points. **Plane:** Any flat surface. **Vertices:** Plural for vertex. The vertex is the point formed when two straight lines meet at an angle. **Perpendicular:** Two lines that form a 90° (90 degree) angle.

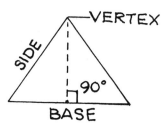

The formula

$$A = \frac{1}{2} \times b \times h$$

is read as:

Area = One-half times Base times Height

The height of a triangle is a straight perpendicular line from a side to a vertex. The side is called the base and a small box is drawn between the height line and the base to indicate that they meet at a 90° angle.

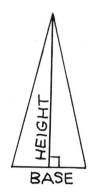

Problems

Question   Find the area of the triangle.

The height is the line that forms a 90° line with the base.

English
Formula: A = ½ × b × h
     Height = 8 in.
      Base = 4 in.
      Area = ½ × 4 in. × 8 in.

When multiplying three numbers together, work with two numbers at a time. Multiply the first two and then multiply the product of these two numbers by the third number.

Think!   ½ × 4 in. = 2 in.
           thus
           A = 2 in. × 8 in. = 16 in.^{2}

Metric
Formula: A = ½ × b × h
     Height = 20 cm
      Base = 10 cm
      Area = ½ × 10 cm × 20 cm

Think!   ½ × 10 cm = 5 cm
           thus
           A = 5 cm × 20 cm = 100 cm^2

Question   Find the area of the triangle.

The height line in this triangle is also one of the sides.

English
Formula: A = ½ × b × h
     Height = 4 in.
      Base = 6 in.
      Area = ½ × 6 in. × 4 in.

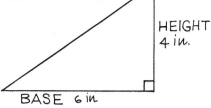

Think!   ½ × 6 in. = 3 in.
              thus
              A = 3 in. × 4 in = 12 in.²

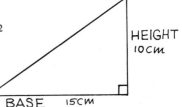

HEIGHT
10 cm

BASE   15 cm

Metric

Formula: A = ½ × b × h
     Height = 10 cm
       Base = 15 cm
       Area = ½ × 15 cm × 10 cm

Think!   ½ × 15 cm = 7.5 cm
              thus
              A = 7.5 cm × 10 cm = 75 cm²

Exercises

1. Find the area of the sail on the boat.

26 ft
(8 m)

13 ft (4 m)

2. Find the area of the sign if it has a height of 15 in. (38 cm) and a base of 10 in. (25 cm).

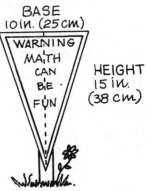

BASE
10 in. (25 cm)

WARNING
MATH
CAN
BE
FUN

HEIGHT
15 in.
(38 cm)

Activity: **EQUALS**

Purpose   To demonstrate how the area formula for triangles, A = ½ × b × h, is determined.

Materials   pencil   red crayon
                ruler   typing paper
                scissors

Procedure

■ Use the pencil to draw two shapes, a 4 in. (10 cm) × 6 in. (15 cm) rectangle, and a 4 in. (10 cm) square.

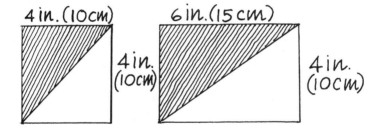

■ Draw a diagonal line across each of the figures.

■ Color one triangle in each figure red, leaving the remaining two triangles uncolored.

■ Use the scissors to cut out the four triangles.

■ Arrange the four pieces to form two separate triangles, one colored and one uncolored.

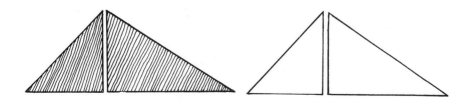

- Compare the sizes of the two triangles.

- Combine two of the four pieces to form one rectangle.

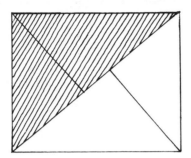

- Rearrange the four pieces to change the size of the rectangle.

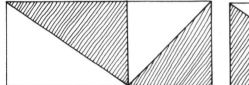 

Results The rectangle is made of two triangles, each with the same total surface area. The area of a rectangle is calculated by using the formula

$$A = \text{Length (Base)} \times \text{Width (Height)}.$$

Since each triangle is one-half the area of the rectangle, the area of each separate triangle can be calculated by multiplying the area of the rectangle by $\frac{1}{2}$. A formula for the area of each triangle would be

$$A = \frac{1}{2} \times \text{Base} \times \text{Height}.$$

Did You Know?

The largest pyramid, Quetzalcoatl, is located in Mexico. This structure is 177 ft (54.5 m) tall with a base area of 45 acres.

Solutions

1.

English

Formula: A = $\frac{1}{2}$ × b × h
      Height = 26 ft
      Base = 13 ft
      Area = $\frac{1}{2}$ × 13 ft × 26 ft

Think! $\frac{1}{2}$ × 13 ft = 6.5 ft
         thus
         A = 6.5 ft × 26 ft = 169 ft^2

Metric

Formula: A = $\frac{1}{2}$ × b × h
      Height = 8 m
      Base = 4 m
      Area = $\frac{1}{2}$ × 4 m × 8 m

Think! $\frac{1}{2}$ × 4 cm = 2 m
         thus
         A = 2 m × 8 m = 16 m^2

2.

English

Formula: A = $\frac{1}{2}$ × b × h
      Height = 15 in.
      Base = 10 in.
      Area = $\frac{1}{2}$ × 10 in. × 15 in.

Think! $\frac{1}{2}$ × 10 in. = 5 in.
         thus
         A = 5 in. × 15 in. = 75 in^2

Metric

Formula: A = $\frac{1}{2}$ × b × h
      Height = 38 cm
      Base = 25 cm
      Area = $\frac{1}{2}$ × 25 cm × 38 cm

Think! $\frac{1}{2}$ × 25 cm = 12.5 cm
         thus
         A = 12.5 cm × 38 cm = 475 cm^2

13
Area of Circles

Purpose To find the area of a circle using the formula $A = \pi r^2$.

Facts The formula $A = \pi r^2$ is read as:

Area = pi times radius times radius

or

pi times radius squared

Since pi (π) is always the same number—3.14—the formula can be written as:

Area = $3.14 \times$ Radius $\times$ Radius = $3.14r^2$

Problems

Question A circular rug has a radius of 7 ft (2 m). What is the surface area of the rug?

English

Formula: $A = \pi \times r \times r$

Radius = 7 ft

= 3.14

$A = 3.14 \times 7$ ft $\times 7$ ft

Think! 3.14×7 ft = 21.98 ft

thus

$A = 21.98$ ft $\times 7$ ft = 153.86 ft^2

When multiplying three numbers together, work with two numbers at a time. Multiply the first two, then multiply the product of these two numbers by the third number.

Metric

Formula: A = π × r × r
    Radius = 2 m
          = 3.14
          A = 3.14 × 2 m × 2 m

Think!   3.14 × 2 m = 6.28 m
             thus
             A = 6.28 m × 2 m = 12.56 m²

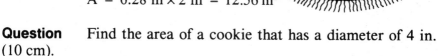

Question   Find the area of a cookie that has a diameter of 4 in.
(10 cm).

English

Formula: A = π × r × r
    Diameter = 4 in.
      Radius = ½ × diameter
            = ½ × 4 in. = 2 in.
         π = 3.14
         A = 3.14 × 2 in. × 2 in.

Think!   3.14 × 2 in. = 6.28 in.
             thus
             A = 6.28 in. × 2 in. = 12.56 in.²

Metric

Formula: A = π × r × r
   Diameter = 10 cm
    Radius = ½ × diameter
         = ½ × 10 cm = 5 cm
       π = 3.14
      A = 3.14 × 5 cm × 5 cm

Think!   3.14 × 5 cm = 15.7 cm
          thus
          A = 15.7 cm × 5 cm = 78.5 cm²

Exercises

1. Determine the area of the lid on the can.

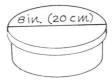

2. The second hand of the clock is 6 in. (15 cm) long. Determine the area that the hand sweeps in 1 minute.

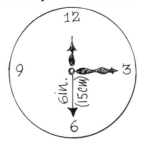

*3 A circle was cut from a 12 in. (30 cm) square of material. How much material was not used?

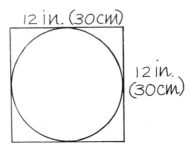

Activity: HOW BIG?

Purpose   To demonstrate the effect a change in radius has on the size of a circle.

Materials   3 circular objects with diameters of approximately 2 in. (5 cm), 4 in. (10 cm), and 6 in. (15 cm) (*Note:* The exact size is not important.)

spool of thread   ruler
pencil   scissors
typing paper   straight pin

Procedure

- Use the circular objects to draw three separate circles on the typing paper with diameters of approximately 2 in. (5 cm), 4 in. (10 cm), and 6 in. (15 cm).

- Use scissors to cut each circle from the paper.

- Stick a straight pin through the center of the smallest circle.

- Place the paper in the palm of your hand with the pin pointing up.

- Remove any paper covering the hole through the thread spool, then position the hole in the spool over the pin.

- While holding the spool, blow into the top of the hole.

- Remove your hand from beneath the paper while continuing to blow through the spool.

- Repeat the procedure using the larger paper circles.

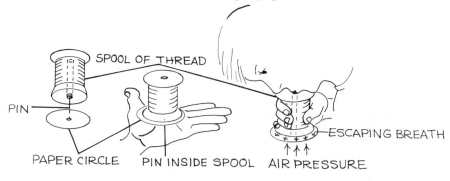

Results   The smaller circles do not fall, but stay on the bottom of the spool. The air flows out between the paper and the spool, producing a low-pressure area. The air beneath the paper pushes up with enough force to keep the paper from falling. The circles finally get too large for the air to hold up. The largest circle falls.

Did You Know?

The largest recorded pizza had a diameter of 1,201 in. (3051 cm). It was cut into 94,248 pieces.

Solutions

1.

English

Formula: $= \pi \times r \times r$
Diameter $= 8$ in.
Radius $= \frac{1}{2} \times$ diameter
         $= \frac{1}{2} \times 8$ in. $= 4$ in.
$\pi = 3.14$
$A = 3.14 \times 4$ in. $\times 4$ in.

Think! 3.14×4 in. $= 12.56$ in.
thus
$A = 12.56$ in. $\times 4$ in. $= 50.24$ in.^{2}

Metric

Formula: $= \pi \times r \times r$
Diameter $= 20$ cm
Radius $= \frac{1}{2} \times$ diameter
         $= \frac{1}{2} \times 20$ cm $= 10$ cm
$\pi = 3.14$
$A = 3.14 \times 10$ cm $\times 10$ cm

Think! 3.14×10 cm $= 31.4$ cm
thus
$A = 31.4$ cm $\times 10$ cm $= 314$ cm^2

2.

English

Formula: $A = \pi \times r \times r$

Radius $= 6$ in.

$A = 3.14 \times 6$ in. $\times 6$ in.

Think! 3.14×6 in. $= 18.84$ in.

thus

$A = 18.84$ in. $\times 6$ in. $= 113.04$ in.^{2}

Metric

Formula: $A = \pi \times r \times r$

Radius $= 15$ cm

$A = 3.14 \times 15$ cm $\times 15$ cm

Think! 3.14×15 cm $= 47.1$ cm

thus

$A = 47.1$ cm $\times 15$ cm $= 706.5$ cm^2

*3. Calculate the area of the 30-cm square of material and subtract the area of the circle to determine the amount of unused material.

English

Formula: $A = $ Length $\times$ Width

Length $= 12$ in.

Width $= 12$ in.

$A = 12$ in. $\times 12$ in.

$= 144$ in.^{2}

Metric

Formula: $A = $ Length $\times$ Width

Length $= 30$ cm

Width $= 30$ cm

$A = 30$ cm $\times 30$ cm

$= 900$ cm^2

English

Formula: $A = \pi \times r \times r$

    Diameter = 12 in.

      Radius = $1/2 \times$ Diameter

            = $1/2 \times 12$ in. = 6 in.

        π = 3.14

        A = 3.14×6 in. $\times 6$ in.

Think! 3.14×6 in. = 18.84 in.

           thus

           A = 18.84 in. $\times 6$ in. = 113.04 in.^{2}

Area of square	=	144.00 in.^{2}
− Area of circle	=	− 113.04 in.^{2}
Unused material	=	30.96 in.^{2}

Metric

Formula: $A = \pi \times r \times r$

    Diameter = 30 cm

      Radius = $1/2 \times$ Diameter

            = $1/2 \times 30$ cm = 15 cm

        π = 3.14

        A = 3.14×15 cm $\times 15$ cm

Think! 3.14×15 cm = 47.1 cm

           thus

           A = 47.1 cm $\times 15$ cm = 706.5 cm^2

Area of square	=	900.0 cm
− Area of circle	=	− 706.5 cm
Unused material	=	193.5 cm^2

14
Surface Area

Purpose   To determine the surface area of objects with different shapes.

Facts   The **surface area** equals the total outside area of an object. The total surface area is the sum of the areas of the box's top, bottom, and four sides. Each of the six parts has the shape of a rectangle, so the area of each part can be determined by using the formula

$$\text{Area} = \text{Length} \times \text{Width}.$$

Problem

Question   Determine the surface area of this closed box.

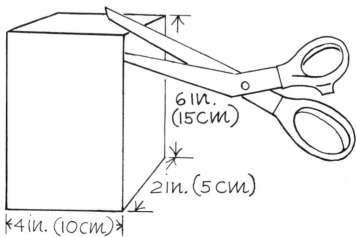

6 in. (15 cm)

2 in. (5 cm)

4 in. (10 cm)

English

Top area	$= 4 \text{ in.} \times 2 \text{ in.} =$	8 in.^2
Bottom area	$= 4 \text{ in.} \times 2 \text{ in.} =$	8 in.^2
Left-side area	$= 2 \text{ in.} \times 6 \text{ in.} =$	12 in.^2
Front area	$= 4 \text{ in.} \times 6 \text{ in.} =$	24 in.^2
Right-side area	$= 2 \text{ in.} \times 6 \text{ in.} =$	12 in.^2
Back area	$= 4 \text{ in.} \times 6 \text{ in.} =$	24 in.^2
Surface area	$=$	88 in.^2

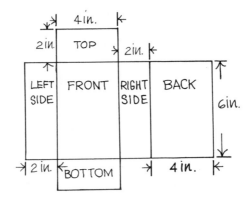

Metric

Top area	$= 10 \text{ cm} \times 5 \text{ cm} =$	50 cm^2
Bottom area	$= 10 \text{ cm} \times 5 \text{ cm} =$	50 cm^2
Left-side area	$= 5 \text{ cm} \times 15 \text{ cm} =$	75 cm^2
Front area	$= 15 \text{ cm} \times 10 \text{ cm} =$	150 cm^2
Right-side area	$= 5 \text{ cm} \times 15 \text{ cm} =$	75 cm^2
Back area	$= 15 \text{ cm} \times 10 \text{ cm} =$	150 cm^2
Surface area	$=$	262 cm^2

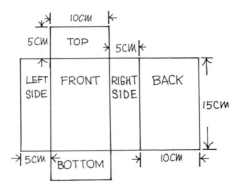

Exercises

1. Determine the surface area of the cereal box.

2. Determine the surface area of the open toy box.

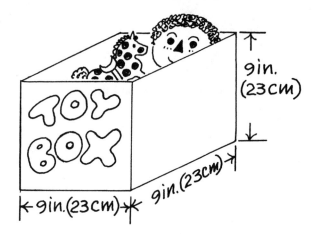

Activity: RAINBOW NECKLACE

Purpose   To demonstrate that surface area can remain the same even though the shape of an object changes.

Materials   notebook paper   pencil
scissors   crayons
ruler

Procedure

- Use a pencil to draw a rectangle on the lined paper that is 4 in. (10 cm) wide and 12 lines long.

- Cut the rectangle from the paper with the scissors.

- Use the crayons to color each of the 12 lines on the rectangle different colors.

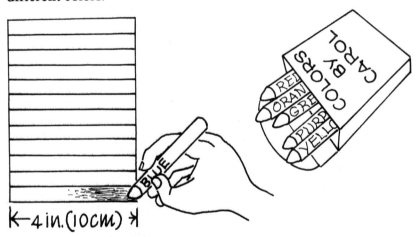

- Fold the rectangle in half along the long side.

- Cut across the fold at points A and B. Stop about ¼ in. (1 cm) from the edge of the paper.

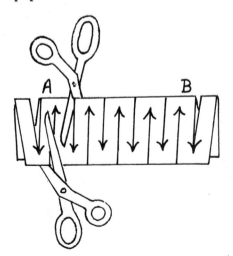

- Notice that all the cuts are along the lines printed on the paper and that each cut stops ¼ in. (1 cm) from the edge. The cuts alternate from the folded edge to the open edge.

- Cut along each of the printed lines alternating from the folded edge to the open edge. Be sure to stop ¼ in. (1 cm) from the edge.

- Start at point A and cut the folded edge off of the paper ending at point B. (*Note:* Do not cut the folded edge from the two end sections.)

- Carefully stretch the paper open and slip the rainbow-colored necklace around your neck.

Results   The shape of the paper changed from a rectangle to a zig-zag chainlike structure, but the surface area of the paper remained the same.

Did You Know?

The small intestine of a human fits snugly inside the abdominal cavity. If this coiled tube is stretched out, its length is about 29 ft (9 m).

Solutions

1.

English

Top area	=	7 in. × 2 in. =	14 in.^{2}
Bottom area	=	7 in. × 2 in. =	14 in.^{2}
Left-side area	=	2 in. × 11 in. =	22 in.^{2}
Front area	=	7 in. × 11 in. =	77 in.^{2}
Right-side area	=	2 in. × 11 in. =	22 in.^{2}
Back area	=	+ 7 in. × 11 in. =	77 in.^{2}
Surface area	=		226 in.^{2}

TOP 2 in. 5 CM 7 in. (18 CM)

LEFT SIDE SNAPPY RIGHT SIDE BACK

CEREAL

SNAP SNAP

2 in. 5 CM BOTTOM 2 in. 5 CM

├─7 in. (18 CM)─┤

Metric

Top area	=	18 cm × 5 cm =	90 cm^2
Bottom area	=	18 cm × 5 cm =	90 cm^2
Left-side area	=	5 cm × 28 cm =	140 cm^2
Front area	=	18 cm × 28 cm =	504 cm^2
Right-side area	=	5 cm × 28 cm =	140 cm^2
Back area	=	+ 18 cm × 28 cm =	504 cm^2
Surface area	=		1468 cm^2

2. The toy box is an open box with five square sides. Since each of the five sides has the same area, the total surface area of the box can be determined by multiplying the area of one of the sides by five.

English
Area of one side $= 9$ in. $\times 9$ in. $= 81$ in.^{2}
Total surface area $= 81$ in.$^2 \times 5 = 405$ in.^{2}

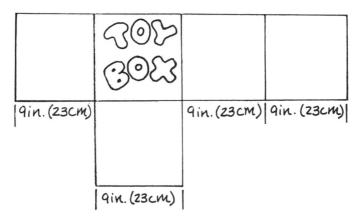

Metric
Area of one side $= 23$ cm $\times 23$ cm $= 529$ cm^2
Total surface area $= 529$ cm$^2 \times 5 = 2645$ cm^2

15

Volume of Cubes and Rectangular Prisms

Purpose   To find the volume of cubes and rectangular prisms using the formula:

Volume $=$ Length $\times$ Width $\times$ Height

The formula is abbreviated

$V = l \times w \times h$

Facts

Cubes and rectangular prisms have three different measurements, length, width, and height. Changing the position of the box does not affect its volume but can change the labeling of the length, width, and height. When three units (such as in. $\times$ in. $\times$ in.) are multiplied, a small 3 is placed to the upper right of the unit (in.^{3}) and the combination is read as inches cubed or cubic inches.

Problems

Question   Find the volume of the box.

English

Volume $=$ Length $\times$ Width $\times$ Height
$= 6$ in. $\times 2$ in. $\times 4$ in.

HEIGHT 4 in.
10 CM

6 in. (15 CM)
LENGTH

2 in.
(5 CM)
WIDTH

When multiplying three numbers together, work with two numbers at a time. Multiply the first two and then multiply the product of these two numbers by the third number.

Think!   6 in. × 2 in. = 12 in.^{2}
       then
       Volume = 12 in.^{2} × 4 in. = 48 in.^{3}

Metric
Volume = Length × Width × Height
       = 15 cm × 5 cm × 10 cm

Think!   15 cm × 5 cm = 75 cm^2
       then
       Volume = 75 cm^2 × 10 cm = 750 cm^3

Question   What is the volume of the box in Problem 1, if it is turned on its end?

English
Volume = Length × Width × Height
       = 4 in. × 2 in. × 6 in.

Think!   4 in. × 2 in. = 8 in.^{2}
       then
       Volume = 8 in.^{2} × 6 in. = 48 in.^{3}

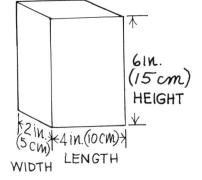

Metric
Volume = Length × Width × Height
       = 10 cm × 5 cm × 15 cm

Think!   10 cm × 5 cm = 50 cm^2
       then
       Volume = 50 cm^2 × 15 cm = 750 cm^3

Note: Changing the position of box did not change the three measurements that were multiplied together, and the order in which the numbers are multiplied does not change the product.

Exercises

1. What is the volume of the room?

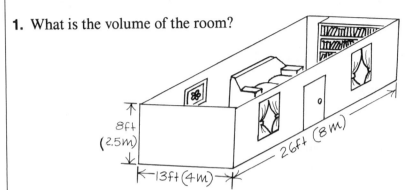

8ft
(2.5m)

26ft (8m)

⟵13ft (4m)⟶

2. Calculate the volume of the picnic cooler.

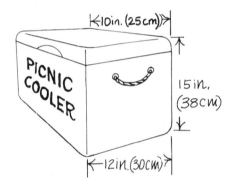

⟵10in. (25cm)⟶

PICNIC COOLER

15in.
(38cm)

⟵12in.(30cm)⟶

*3. A pitcher holding 122 in.^{3} (2000 cm^3) of water is used to fill an aquarium. Would 25 pitchers of water fill the aquarium?

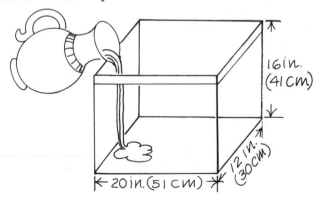

16in.
(41cm)

12in.
(30cm)

⟵20in.(51cm)⟶

Activity: MEASURING BOX

Purpose   To determine how much water a 4 in. (10 cm) cube will hold.

Materials   pencil   glue, white, all purpose
ruler   scissors
stiff paper, such as a file folder
1 qt (1 liter) soda bottle, empty
bowl large enough to hold the box

Procedure

■ On the stiff paper, draw a full-sized enlargement of the pattern shown using your ruler.

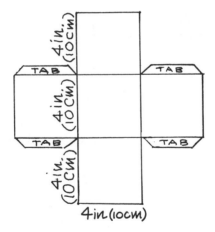

■ Cut out the drawing and fold to make a cube with 4 in. (10 cm) sides.

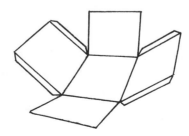

- Use the glue to secure the tabs.
- Cover the seams inside the box with a generous layer of glue to make the box leakproof.
- Allow the glue to thoroughly dry.
- Fill the 1 qt (1 liter) bottle with water.
- Place the box in a bowl to catch any water spills.

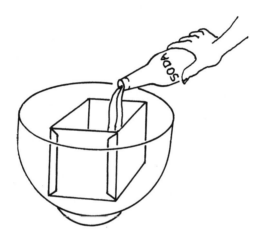

- Slowly pour the water from the bottle into the box until the box is overflowing.

Results   The box will hold 1 qt (1 liter) of water. A 4 in. (10 cm) cube has a volume of 64 in.^{3} (1000 cm^3). This volume equals 1 qt (1 liter).

Did You Know?

The largest box of popcorn measured 25 ft (7.7 m) x 25 ft (7.7 m) x 6.06 ft (1.86 m). The box was filled by Jones High School, Orlando, Florida, Dec 15–17, 1988.

Solutions

1.

English
Volume = Length × Width × Height
= 13 ft × 26 ft × 8 ft

Think!   13 ft × 26 ft = 338 ft^2
then
Volume = 338 ft^2 × 8 ft = 2704 ft^3

Metric
Volume = Length × Width × Height
= 4 m × 8 m × 2.5 m

Think!   4 m × 8 m = 32 m^2
then
Volume = 32 m^2 × 2.5 m = 80 m^3

2.

English
Volume = Length × Width × Height
= 12 in. × 10 in. × 15 in.

Think!   12 in. × 10 in. = 120 in.^{2}
then
Volume = 120 in.^{2} × 15 in. = 1800 in.^{3}

Metric
Volume = Length × Width × Height
= 30 cm × 25 cm × 38 cm

Think!   30 cm × 25 cm = 750 cm^2
then
Volume = 750 cm^2 × 38 cm = 28,500 cm^3

3.

English

1 pitcher $=$ 122 in.^{3}

25 pitchers $= 25 \times 122$ in.^{3}

$= 3,050$ in.^{3}

3,050 in.^{3} is less than the 3,840 in.^{3} volume of the aquarium.

Metric

1 pitcher $=$ 2,000 cm^3

25 pitchers $= 25 \times 2,000$ cm^3

$= 50,000$ cm^3

50,000 cm^3 is less than the 62,730 cm^3 volume of the aquarium.

Answer No, 25 pitchers of water will not fill the aquarium.

16
Volume by Displacement

Purpose To calculate the volume of an object by water displacement.

Facts When an object is placed into a container of water, the amount of water the object pushes out of its way is equal to its **volume**. The water is being **displaced**, pushed aside, by the object; the object's volume is thus determined by the amount of water it displaces.

Problem

Question A rock is placed in 50 qt (50 liters) of water. The water level rises to 60 qt. (60 liters). What is the volume of the rock?

$$
\begin{array}{lcr}
\text{Water volume} + \text{Rock volume} & = & 60 \text{ qt (liters)} \\
- \text{Water volume} & = & -50 \text{ qt (liters)} \\
\hline
\text{Rock volume} & = & 10 \text{ qt (liters)}
\end{array}
$$

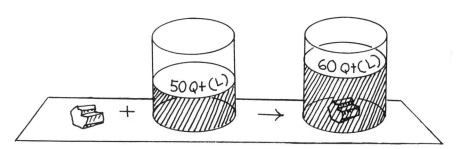

Exercises

1. What is the volume of the fish?

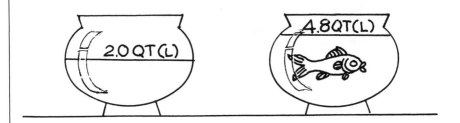

2. How much of the water is displaced by the toy diver?

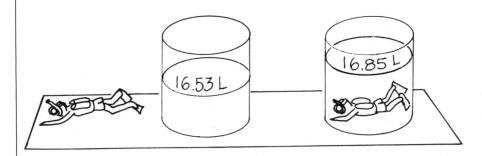

*3. Each metal ball displaces 0.1 qt (0.1 liter). Study the picture to determine the number of balls in the jar.

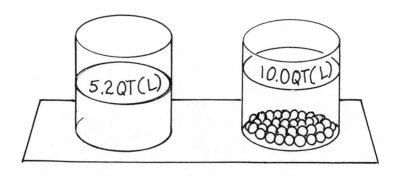

Activity: SAME SIZE?

Purpose   To compare the volume of your hands.

Materials   2 rubber bands   marking pen
                 fish bowl   helper
                 masking tape

Procedure

- Place a strip of tape down the side of the fish bowl.

- Fill the bowl three-quarters full with water.

- Use the pen to mark the water level on the tape. Label this starting mark with the letter S.

- Slip one rubber band around each of your wrists at exactly the same place. (*Note:* Be sure the rubber bands *do not* cut off your circulation. They should not be so tight as to cause the skin to pucker.)

- Push your left hand into the water until the rubber band is touching the surface of the water.

- Ask your helper to mark the level of the water on the tape and label the mark with the letter L.

- Remove your hand and add water to bring the level back to the starting mark, S.

- Push your right hand into the water until the rubber band touches the surface of the water.

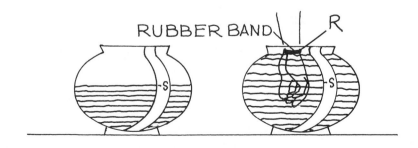

RUBBER BAND   R

■ Have your helper mark the level of the line on the tape with the letter R.

Results   The lines R and L are very close together or possibly the letters are at the same position. Each hand pushes the water out of its way as it enters the liquid. The volume of each hand is equal to the amount of water it displaces. Your hands are not exactly the same, but the measuring instrument in this experiment is not sensitive enough to indicate small differences, so equal volumes for your hands may be shown. Volumes of objects such as hands, rocks, pieces of gold, or any irregular-shaped objects can be determined by water displacement.

Did You Know?

The weight of the water that your hands displaced is about the same as the weight of your hands. This is because the weight of the human body is about the same as an equal volume of water.

Solutions

1.   Water volume + Fish   =   4.8 qt (liters)
– Water volume   = – 2.0 qt (liters)
Fish volume   =   2.8 qt (liters)

2.   Water volume + Volume of toy diver = 16.85 qt (liters)
– Water volume   = 16.53 qt (liters)
Volume of diver   =   0.32 qt (liters)

*3.   Water volume + Balls =   10.0 qt (liters)
– Water volume   = –   5.2 qt (liters)
Volume of balls   =   4.8 qt (liters)

To determine the number of balls, divide the displaced volume of all the balls by the volume of 1 ball.

4.8 qt (liters) ÷ 0.1 qt (liter) = 48 balls

17
Liquid Capacity

Purpose   To measure and determine equivalent liquid capacities.

Facts

Unit	Abbreviation	Equivalent Measurements
quart	qt	1 liter = 1 qt
liter	L	1 liter = 1000 ml
milliliter	ml	1 liter = 4 cups
cup	c	1 cup = 250 ml
tablespoon	T	1 T = 15 ml
teaspoon	tsp	1 tsp = 5 ml

Problem

Question   A pitcher contains 2 qt (2 liters) of lemonade. How many cups (250 ml) can be filled with the lemonade?

Facts:
$$2 \text{ qt} = 2 \text{ liters}$$
$$2 \text{ liters} = 2000 \text{ ml}$$
$$1 \text{ cup} = 250 \text{ ml}$$
$$? \text{ cups} = 2000 \text{ ml}$$

Think!
$$250 \text{ ml} \times ? = 2000 \text{ ml}$$
$$250 \text{ ml} \times 8 = 2000 \text{ ml}$$

Answer   8 cups

Exercises

1. Rewrite Kimberly's recipe for chocolate milk using milliliter measuring units.

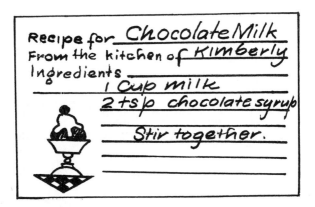

Recipe for Chocolate Milk
From the kitchen of Kimberly
Ingredients
   1 cup milk
   2 tsp chocolate syrup
   Stir together.

2. Jennifer makes a 2 qt pitcher of orange juice by combining 500 ml of orange juice concentrate and water. How much water was added to fill the pitcher?

*3. Lauren has been asked to pour 5 liters of water into the fishbowl by using the unmarked buckets. Describe a method that she can use to measure the liquid.

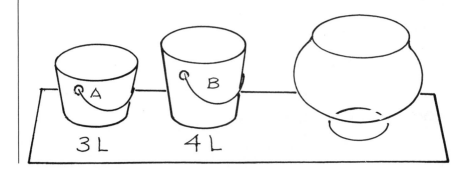

Activity: THE GLOB

Purpose   To measure and use equivalent capacities.

GLOB SOLUTIONS

sodium borate solution
    15 ml sodium borate + 1 liter water
liquid adhesive solution
    18 ml liquid adhesive + 18 ml water

EQUIVALENT GLOB SOLUTIONS

borax solution
    1 T borax + 1 quart water
glue solution
    4 fl oz glue + 4 fl oz water

Materials   borax (sodium borate), found in supermarket with washing detergents
4 fluid oz bottle of liquid glue, white all-purpose

1 measuring spoon, tablespoon (15 ml)	distilled water 2-qt (2-liter) bowl
1 measuring cup, 250 ml capacity	marking pen 2 clean, empty quart (liter)
2 resealable plastic bags	jars, with one tight-fitting lid

Procedure

■ Make a borax solution by filling one of the qt (liter) jars with water. Label the jar Borax with the marking pen. Add 1 T (15 ml) of borax to the water. Put the lid on the jar and shake vigorously.

■ Make a glue solution by emptying a 4 fluid oz bottle of glue into a second jar, labeled Glue. Fill the empty glue bottle with distilled water and pour the water into the jar. [Or measure out 4 ounces (120 ml) of glue and 4 ounces (120 ml) of water.] With a clean spoon, stir until the glue is thoroughly mixed.

■ Pour 1 measuring cup (250 ml) of the borax solution into the empty bowl.

■ Slowly pour the glue solution into the bowl containing the borax. Stir as you pour.

■ Use the stirring spoon to dip the glob out of the bowl.

■ Place the glob on top of a plastic bag for 2 minutes.

■ Pick the glob up with your fingers and squeeze.

■ Transfer the glob from one hand to the other, and squeeze until it and your hands are dry.

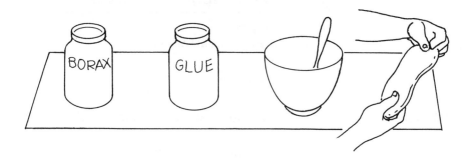

■ Squeeze it! Pull it! Stretch it! Have fun with it!

■ Place the glob inside the plastic bag and seal to store.

■ Wash your hands when you are finished.

Results   A white, pliable glob is formed that stretches and breaks easily when pulled apart sharply but flows if placed where gravity is the acting force.

You can make different colored globs by adding a drop of food coloring to the glue-water mixture.

Solutions

1. Facts   1 cup = 250 ml
        1 tsp = 5 ml

  Think!   1 cup milk = 250 ml milk
     2 tsp = 2×5 ml = 10 ml chocolate syrup

2. Facts:
        1 qt = 1 liter
       1 liter = 1000 ml

  Think!   2 qt = 2 liters
      2 liters = 2000 ml

  Think! Volume of pitcher – Volume juice = Volume of water
        2000 ml – 500 ml = 1500 ml

  Answer   1500 ml of water

*3. Facts:
  1. Fill Bucket B with 4 liters of water.
  2. Fill Bucket A with 3 liters of water from Bucket B.
  3. Pour the 1 liter of water left in Bucket B into the fish bowl.
  4. Fill Bucket B again and pour the 4 liters of water into the fishbowl to make a total of 5 liters.

18
Mass

Purpose   To become more familiar with metric units and choose equivalent metric mass measurements.

Facts   Milligram (mg), centigram (cg), gram (g), and kilogram (kg) are metric units used to measure mass.

$$1000 \text{ milligrams (mg)} = 1 \text{ gram (g)}$$
$$100 \text{ centigrams (cg)} = 1 \text{ gram (g)}$$
$$1000 \text{ grams (g)} = 1 \text{ kilogram (kg)}$$

Problem

Question   Choose the object that you think will balance the measured mass on the scale.

You must first make mental comparisons of the mass of each of the three objects. Which one has the greatest, medium, or least mass? Now evaluate the mass on the scale. Is 7 kg a large, medium, or small mass? Since kilogram is the largest of the three mass units used in this exercise, find an object that has a large amount of mass, such as the bowling ball.

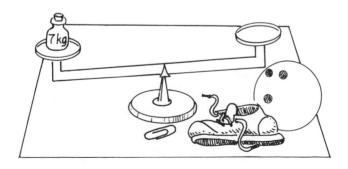

Exercises

1. Which object has a 5 g mass?

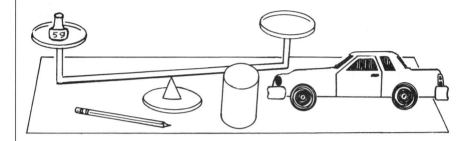

2. Which of the bags will balance the child on the seesaw?

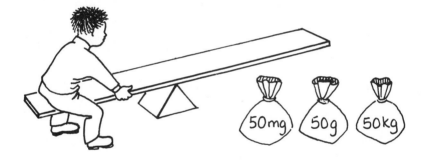

*3. How many boxes of paper clips are needed to balance the 1500 g pot of flowers?

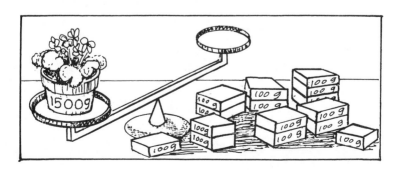

Activity: **BALANCED**

Purpose   To make and use a balance to compare metric masses.

Materials   clothes hanger with   heavy book
                     paper rod   scissors
                 2 paper cups   ruler
                 string   small paper clips
                 pencil   coin

Procedure

■ Cut two 12 in. (30 cm) lengths of string.

■ Use the point of the pencil to make two holes in each of the paper cups. The holes should be near the top and on opposite sides of the cups.

■ On each cup, tie one end of a 12 in. (30 cm) string in each hole to form a loop.

■ Remove and discard the paper holder from the clothes hanger.

■ Place the book on the edge of a table.

■ Slip the end of the pencil under the book, leaving most of the pencil hanging over the edge of the table.

■ Hang the clothes hanger on the pencil.

■ Hang the string of each cup on one hook of the clothes hanger.

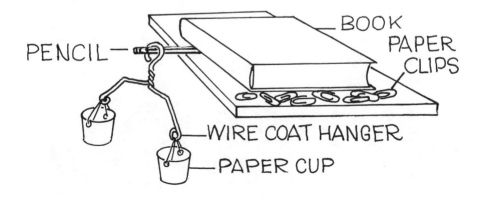

- Bend the wire arms up or down to make the two paper cups hang level.

- Place a coin in the left cup.

- Add paper clips to the right cup, one at a time, until the cups again are level.

Results   The cups and string have an equal mass and balance on the arms of the clothes hanger. The number of paper clips needed to balance the coin will depend on the mass of the coin that you use.

Did You Know?

The brachiosaurus is believed to have been about 39 ft (12 m) tall, 75 ft (23 meters) long, and have a mass of 45,000 kg.

Solutions

1. Order   Largest mass = Car
                Medium mass = Can of soup
                Least mass = Pencil

    Think!   5 grams is a small mass. A paper clip masses about 1 g, which object would be about the same mass as five paper clips?

    Answer Pencil

2. Order   Largest mass = 50 kg
                Medium mass = 50 g
                Least mass = 50 mg

    Think!   50 mg is the mass of about 5 fleas, and 50 g equals the mass of 50 paper clips. The child would be balanced by the bag massing 50 kg.

    Answer 50-kg bag

*3. *Think!*   One box of paper clips = 100 g

Mass of flower pot = 1500 g

Mass of one box x Number of boxes = Mass of flower pot

100 g   x   ?   = 1500 g

100 g   x   15 boxes = 1500 g

Answer 15 boxes

19
Weight

Purpose   To become more familiar with the weight measurements of ton, pound, and ounce.

Facts   16 ounces (oz) = 1 pound (lb)
                 2000 pound (lb) = 1 ton (T)

Reference items:

Small car = 1 ton
Loaf of bread = 1 lb
Slice of cheese = 1 oz

Problem

Question   Choose the item that weighs closest to 16 pounds.

Question   Mentally label the objects as largest, medium, and least weight. Compare each object with some known reference such as those in the Facts section of this exercise. Now evaluate the weight of 16 lb, which is the weight of 16 loaves of bread. The most likely choice would be the bicycle.

Exercises

1. Which object weighs 2 ounces?

2. Choose the object that weighs 8 pounds.

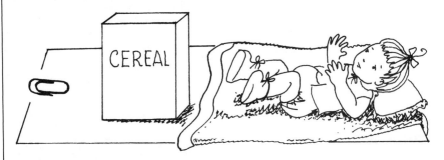

3. What is the weight of the elephant?

    a. 2 tons

    b. 2 ounces

    c. 2 pounds

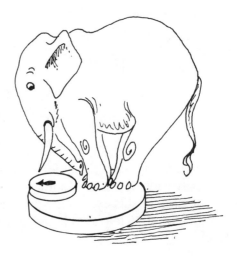

*4. Three kittens were placed inside a basket to weigh them. If the empty basket weighs 4 pounds, how much does each kitten weigh, assuming they have equal weights?

Activity: FORCES

Purpose   To demonstrate forces that affect weight.

Materials   large rock (a brick   scissors
                    will work)   rubber band
                string   bucket

Procedure

■ Fill the bucket ¾ full with water.

■ Tie the string around the rock.

■ Cut the rubber band to form one long strip.

■ Tie one end of the rubber band securely to the string around the rock.

- Hold the free end of the rubber band and slowly pull upward until the rock is suspended.

- Observe the length of the rubber band.

- Slowly lower the rock into the bucket of water until it is suspended about in the middle of the water.

- Again observe the length of the rubber band.

Results   The rubber band is much longer when the rock is suspended in the air than when it is in water. A force called **gravity** pulls the rock toward the earth; the amount of this pull is called the weight of the rock. The upward push of air changes the weight some, but the upward push of the water makes a more noticeable change in the weight of the rock.

Did You Know?

Weight is a result of the pull of gravity. Other celestial bodies have gravity, but in varying amounts. The chart indicates a person's weight on different bodies in our solar system.

Where	Weight
Earth	100 lb
Moon	17 lb
Sun	27,900 lb
Mars	38 lb

Divide your weight by 6 to determine your weight on the moon.

Solutions

1. Order   Largest weight = Hippopotamus
Medium weight = Jar of jelly
Least weight = Slice of bread

Think!   2 oz is a small weight. A slice of cheese weighs 1 oz. Which object weighs the same as two slices of cheese?

Answer   The slice of bread.

2. Order   Largest weight = Baby
Medium weight = Cereal
Least weight = Paperclip

Think!   The ton unit will not be used since none of the three objects weights as much as a car. This leaves the pound and ounce units as choices for each object's weight. Since a loaf of bread weighs 1 lb, which of the three items weighs as much as 8 loaves of bread?

Answer   The baby.

3. Order   Largest weight = 2 tons
Medium weight = 2 lb
Least weight = 2 oz

Think!   You know that 2 oz is the weight of two slices of cheese and that two loaves of bread weigh 2 lb.

Answer   The elephant must weigh 2 tons.

4.   Weight of the basket + Weight of the three kittens =   10 lb
    − Weight of the basket   =   − 4 lb
     Weight of the three kittens   =   6 lb

Think!   Weight of the three kittens = 6 lb
Weight of 3 kittens × ? lbs = 6 lb
3 × 2 lb = 6 lb

Answer   Each kitten weighs 2 lb.

20
Temperature

Purpose   To read Fahrenheit and Celsius thermometers.

Facts   The two types of thermometers used in this exercise are Celsius and Fahrenheit. Notice that the Fahrenheit scale has five divisions between each printed number. Each division equals 2 degrees. There are 10 divisions between each printed number on the Celsius scale. Each division equals 1 degree. The 5th mark on the Celsius scale is longer to make it simpler for you to find the mid-point.

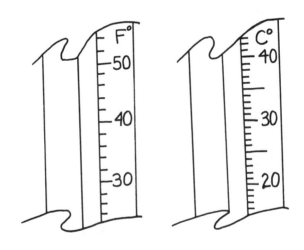

The symbol for the word degree is a small raised circle. °F is read as degrees Fahrenheit and °C is read as degrees Celsius.

Examples: 30°C is read as 30 degrees Celsius
40°F is read as 40 degrees Fahrenheit

Problem

Question   Take temperature readings from the two thermometers.

Think!   **Fahrenheit Scale**
The height of the liquid in the thermometer is at the third mark above 50°F. Each mark equals 2°F.

Thus, the reading on the thermometer is 56°F.

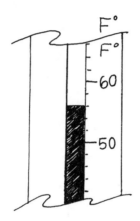

Celsius Scale
The height of the liquid in the thermometer is at the fifth mark above 10°C. Each mark equals 1°C.

Thus, the reading on the thermometer is 15°C.

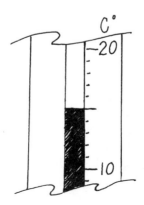

Exercises

1. Read the thermometer.

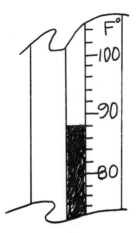

2. Read the thermometer.

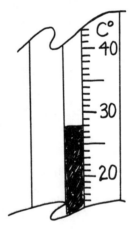

3. Which thermometer reads 10.5°C?

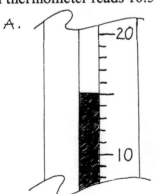

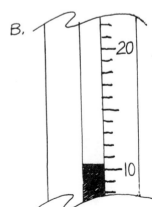

4. Which thermometer reads 69°F?

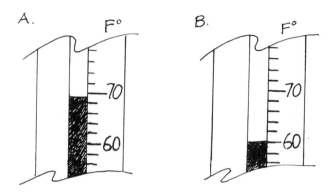

5. Use the labels on the diagram to find the temperature of each of the following.

a. Body temperature of humans in degrees Celsius

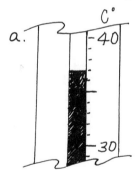

b. Body temperature of humans in degrees Fahrenheit

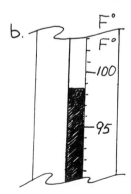

Activity: STRAW THERMOMETER

Purpose   To demonstrate how a thermometer works.

Materials   blue food coloring   2 soup bowls large enough
straw, small, with   to hold the bottle
little or no color   2 ice cubes
modeling clay,   glass soda bottle
walnut-sized piece   measuring cup (250 ml)

Procedure

■ Half fill the measuring cup (125 ml) with water.

■ Add drops of blue food coloring to the water and stir. Continue adding the coloring until the water is deep blue.

■ Place the end of the straw into the colored water.

■ While the straw is in the water, place your index finger over the open end of the straw.

■ Hold the straw closed with your finger while lifting the straw out of the colored water and inserting the free end in the empty soda bottle.

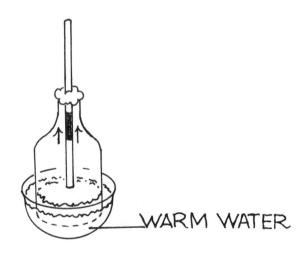

WARM WATER

■ Using your other hand, seal around the mouth of the bottle with clay before removing your finger from the end of the straw.

■ The colored water plug will move up the straw when you release the end. If it comes out the top, try again. If it falls out the bottom, use a straw with a smaller diameter. You want the water to stay in the straw.

■ Fill one of the soup bowls half full with warm water from the faucet.

■ The second bowl is to be filled half full with cold water from the faucet. Add the two ice cubes to this water.

■ Place the empty soda bottle with the straw in the warm water.

■ Remove the bottle from the water when the colored water in the straw starts to move.

■ Place the bottle in the ice water.

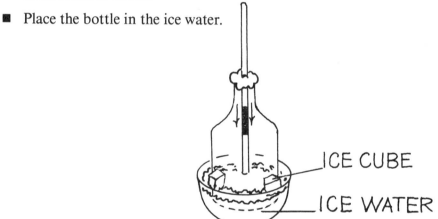

ICE CUBE

ICE WATER

■ Again remove the bottle when the colored water in the straw starts to move.

Results   The colored water moves up when the bottle is placed in warm water and down when the bottle is in cold water. The air inside the bottle expands when heated. This expanding gas pushes the colored water up the straw. Cooling the air inside the bottle causes it to contract, and the air above the straw pushes the colored water downward. Liquids inside thermometers are in a closed tube. When the liquid is heated, it expands and moves up. Cooling the liquid causes contraction, and the liquid moves down the tube.

Did You Know?

The average person has a body temperature of 98.6°F (37°C). A human cannot live with a body temperature above 109°F (42.8°C) or lower than 95°F (35°C). Marathon runners in hot weather have been known to attain body temperatures of 105.8°F (41.°C).

Solutions

1. *Think!*   The height of the liquid in the thermometer is at the fourth mark above 80°F. Each mark equals 2°F.

Thus, the reading on the thermometer is 88°F.

2. *Think!*   The height of the liquid in the thermometer is at the eighth mark above 20°C. Each mark equals 1°C.

Thus, the reading on the thermometer is 28°C.

3. Thermometer B reads 10.5°C.

    Think!   The height of the liquid in thermometer A is at the fifth mark above 10°C. Since each mark equals 1°C the temperature reading is 15°C.

The height of the liquid in thermometer B is halfway between 10°C and 11°C and can be read as 10½ or 10.5°C.

4. Thermometer A reads 69°F.

    Think!   The height of the liquid in thermometer A is halfway between 68°F and 70°F and is read as 69°F.

The height of the liquid in thermometer B is halfway to the first mark. Since each mark equals 2 degrees, the temperature would be a little less than 61°F. or about 60.9°F.

5. a. Body temperature of humans = 37°C.

  b. Body temperature of humans = 98.6°F.

III
Graphing

21
Bar Graph

Purpose   To interpret information on a bar graph.

Facts   Bar graphs make comparing information easier. Each box on the graph has the same value, and the starting value is always 0, not 1.

Problem

Question   Use the horizontal bar graph to answer Questions 1 through 5.

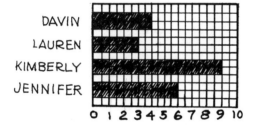

AGES
OF
CHILDREN

1. Who is older, Davin or Jennifer?

2. Which children are older than Davin?

3. Name the children who are younger than Jennifer.

4. Who is the oldest?

5. List the ages of the children.
   The numbering on the horizontal scale indicates that a length of 2 boxes equals 1 year. A length of one box would then equal ½ of a year.

1. *Think!*   Who has the longer bar, Davin or Jennifer?

    Answer   Jennifer

2. *Think*   Who has bars longer than Davin's bar?

    Answer   Kimberly and Jennifer

3. *Think!*   Who has bars shorter than Jennifer's bar?

    Answer   Davin and Lauren

4. *Think!*   Who has the longest bar?

    Answer   Kimberly

5. *Think!*   Start at the right end of each child's bar, and follow the line it touches all the way to the bottom to find the number on the scale.

    Answer
Davin   4 years
Lauren   3 years
Kimberly   9 years
Jennifer   6 years

Exercises

1. Use the following bar graph to answer Questions a through f. Determine all speeds in miles per hour and in kilometers per hour.

   a. How much speed does each square measure?

   b. Which is the fastest animal?

   c. What is the difference in the speed of the lion and the cat?

   d. How many animals are slower than man?

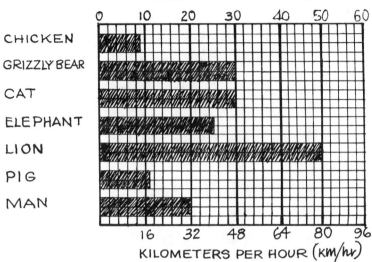

AVERAGE SPEED OF ANIMALS

MILES PER HOUR (MPH)

e. Which animals have the same speed?

f. How many animals are faster than the pig?

2. Use the following bar graph to answer Questions a through f.

   a. How many years does each square measure?

   b. Which animal has the shortest life span?

   c. How many animals live longer than a zebra?

   d. How many years longer does the bear live than the pig?

   e. Which animal lives twice as long as the rabbit?

   f. How many animals have the same life span as a dog?

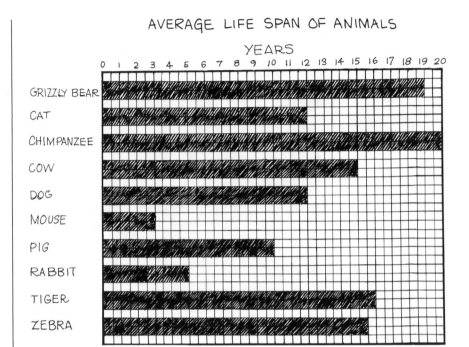

AVERAGE LIFE SPAN OF ANIMALS

Activity: BEAN GROWTH

Purpose   To graph the growth of a bean.

Materials   4 pinto beans   ruler
                paper towels   note pad
                masking tape   pencil
                1 drinking glass

Procedure

■ Fold a paper towel, and line the inside of the glass with it.

■ Wad sheets of paper towels and stuff them into the glass to hold the paper lining tightly against the glass.

■ Place the beans between the paper lining and the glass. The beans should be evenly spaced and about 1 in. (2.5 cm) from the top of the glass.

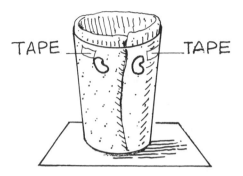

■ Moisten the paper towels in the glass with water. You do not want the paper to be dripping wet, only moist.

■ Keep the paper moist and observe each day until the beans start to grow.

■ When the first sign of a leaf appears, place a piece of tape on the outside of the glass to mark the position of the top of the leaf. The tape marks the beginning of the growth measurements.

■ Measure the growth from the tip of the leaf to the top of the tape after 24 hours (1 day). Record as the growth for day 1.

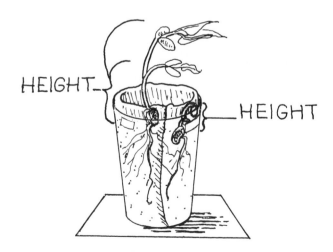

- Continue to measure and record the growth for 7 days.

- Use the measurements to construct a bar graph.

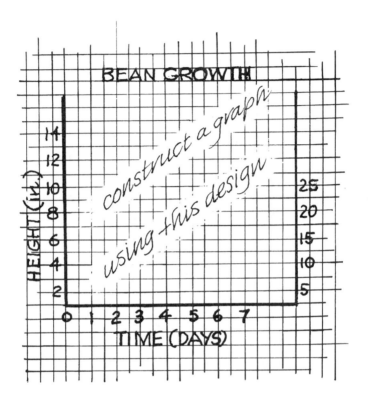

Results   It takes about 7 days before the bean starts to grow. Within another 7 days, the plant growth is very quick. Many centimeters of growth can occur overnight. The bar graph provides an easy way to picture determine how fast the bean grows each day.

Did You Know?

The tallest recorded height of a sunflower plant is 24 ft 2¹/₂ in. (7.45 m).

Solutions

1. a. The numbering on the horizontal scales indicate that each square equals 2 mph (3.2 km/hr).

  b. *Think!*   Which animal has the longer bar?

     Answer   Lion

  c. *Think!*   Start at the right end of the bars for the lion and the cat. Follow the lines up and down to find the numbers on the scales.

$$\begin{array}{rl} \text{Speed of the lion} = & 50 \text{ mph } (80 \text{ km})/\text{hr} \\ - \text{ Speed of the cat} = & -30 \text{ mph } (48 \text{ km})/\text{hr} \\ \hline \text{Difference} = & 20 \text{ mph } (32 \text{ km})/\text{hr} \end{array}$$

     Answer   The lion can run 20 mph (32 km/hr) faster than a cat.

  d. *Think!*   How many bars are shorter than the one for man?

     Answer   Two; the chicken and the pig

  e. *Think!*   How many bars are exactly the same length?

     Answer   Two; the bear and the cat

  f. *Think!*   How many bars are longer than that of the pig?

     Answer   Five; the bear, cat, elephant, lion, and man

2. a. Each square measures one half year.

  b. *Think!*   Which bar is closest to the left?

     Answer   Mouse

c. *Think!*   How many bars are farther to the right than is the bar representing zebras?

Answer   Three; the bear, chimpanzee, and tiger

d. Determine the life span of the bear and the pig by following each bar to the right and then down to the scale. Take the difference between the numbers.

$$
\begin{array}{rr}
\text{Life span of the bear} = & 19 \text{ years} \\
- \text{ Life span of the pig} = & -10 \text{ years} \\
\hline
\text{Difference} = & 9 \text{ years}
\end{array}
$$

Answer   The bear lives 9 years longer than the pig.

e. Determine the life span of the rabbit by following the rabbit's bar to the right and then down to the scale.

Life span of the rabbit = 5 years

Multiply the rabbit's life span by 2.

2×5 years = 10 years

Find 10 years on the scale and move upward until you reach a bar that ends on the 10-year line.

Answer   Pig

f. *Think!*   How many bars extend to the right exactly the same distance as that of the dog?

Answer   One; the bar of the cat

22
Line Graph

Purpose   To interpret information on a line graph.

Facts   Information is recorded as points on the graph. A line is formed by joining the points in order starting on the left and moving to the right. It is not always necessary to start from zero on a line graph.

Problem

Question   For one week, Jennifer took a daily math test. The scores from these tests are recorded on the line graph. Use the graph to answer Questions 1 through 3.

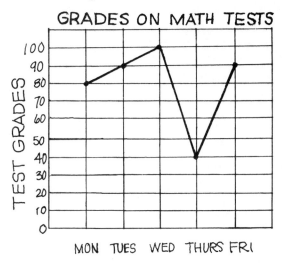

1. On which day did Jennifer know the most answers?

2. On which day did she know the fewest answers?

3. On which night did Jennifer watch television instead of studying for her math test?

1. *Think!*   Which day has the highest point on the line?

    Answer   Wednesday

2. *Think!*   Which day has the lowest point on the line?

    Answer   Thursday

3. *Think!*   Thursday was the day she scored the lowest grade. We can thus assume that she watched television on Wednesday night instead of preparing for her test.

    Answer: Wednesday night

Exercises

1. Robert buys candy with his allowance money. The number of candy bars he ate during 1 week is recorded on the line graph. Use the graph to answer Questions a through d.

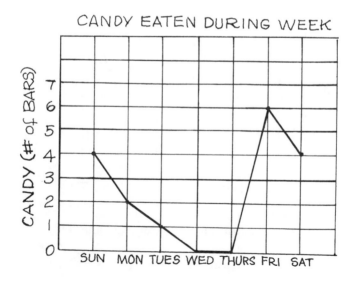

CANDY EATEN DURING WEEK

a. On which day were the most candy bars eaten?

b. On which days were more than three bars of candy eaten?

c. How many days did Robert not eat candy?

d. How many bars of candy did Robert eat during the week?

2. Russell timed his pulse rate before and after exercising to determine his recovery pulse rate, the time it took for his pulse rate to
return to normal. His pulse rates are recorded on the line graph.
Use the graph to answer Questions a through d.

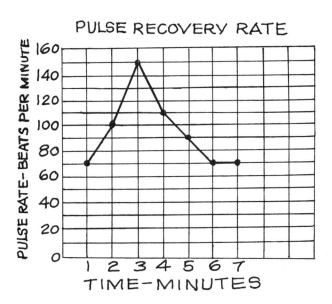

a. What is Russell's normal pulse rate?

b. How long did he exercise?

c. What was his highest pulse rate?

d. How long did it take his pulse to return to normal?

Activity: HOW FAST?

Purpose   To use a distance versus time line graph to compare the speed of a moving object at different times.

Materials   ruler   notebook paper
                book   marble
                timer, second hand   pencil
                   on a watch   helper

Procedure

- Place 6 sheets of paper on the floor to form a long path.

- Position the book on the edge of the paper trail.

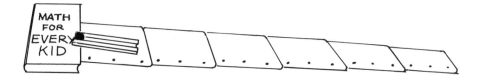

- Rest one end of the ruler on the edge of the book and the other end on the paper.

- Hold the marble at the top of the ruler.

- Release the marble, allowing it to roll down the center groove in the ruler.

- Your helper should be ready with a pencil to mark the position of the marble as it rolls across the paper.

- Start timing as soon as the marble touches the paper.

- Count aloud the passing of each second until 4 seconds have passed.

- As each second is announced, your helper should mark on the paper the position of the marble.

- Measure and record the inch and centimeter distances from the end of the ruler to each mark.

DATA TABLE #1

TIME SECONDS	DISTANCE INCHES	SPEED IN SECONDS

DATA TABLE #2

TIME SECONDS	DISTANCE INCHES	SPEED IN SECONDS

■ Plot the data on a line graph. Use a solid line to connect inch measurements and a dashed line for the centimeter distances.

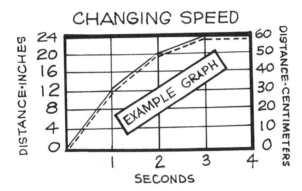

■ Observe the steepness of the lines between points.

Results   The marble moves a greater distance during the first second because it is traveling at a faster speed. The speed decreases until finally the marble stops. This decrease in speed is indicated by the decrease in distance traveled. The height of the line between points indicates the speed. The steeper the line, the faster the speed. A horizontal line indicates no change in distance, thus a speed of zero.

Did You Know?

The marble slows and stops due to friction. Friction is a resistance to movement. Without friction, the marble would have continued to move until it hit another object. This is what happens to moving objects in space.

Solutions

1. a. *Think!*   Which day has the highest point on the line?

   Answer   Friday

   b. *Think!*   Which days have points higher than the horizontal line representing 3 candy bars?

   Answer   Sunday, Friday, and Saturday

   c. *Think!*   Which days have points on the horizontal line representing 0 candy bars?

   Answer   Two; Wednesday and Thursday

   d. *Think!*   How many candy bars did he eat each day? Add them up to find how many he ate that week.

   Answer $4 + 2 + 1 + 6 + 4 = 17$

2. a. *Think!*   What was the beginning and ending pulse rate?

   Answer   70 beats per minute

   b. *Think!*   When did the rate start to increase and when did it stop? It began increasing at 1 minute and stopped increasing at 3 minutes. How many minutes passed between these points?

   Answer   Two minutes

   c. *Think!*   What is the highest point on the line? Follow this point to the left scale and read the number.

   Answer   150 beats per minute

d. *Think!*   At what time did the rate start to change and when did it return to normal—70 beats per minute? It started increasing at 1 minute and returned at 6 minutes. How long between these time periods?

Answer   5 minutes

23

Pictograph

Purpose   To interpret and construct pictographs.

Facts   Pictographs contain symbols that represent a specific number of objects. In the problem below, a book is used as a symbol to represent 10 books that had been read. Pictographs are fun and easy to read. Symbols show data involving large or small numbers.

Problem

Question   The number of books read by five different people was recorded on a pictograph. Use the pictograph to answer Questions 1 through 3.

NAME	BOOKS READ IN ONE YEAR EACH 📖 STANDS FOR 10 BOOKS
RYAN	📖 📖 📖
KIMBERLY	📖 📖 📖 📖 📖
DAVIN	📖
JENNIFER	📖 📖 📖
LAUREN	📖 📖

a. Who read the fewest books?

b. How many books did Jennifer read?

c. How many more books must Davin read to equal the books read by Jennifer?

a. ***Think!***   Which name has the fewest book symbols?

   Answer   Davin

b. ***Think!***   How many symbols follow Jennifer's name? There are $2\frac{1}{2}$ symbols. The half symbol would equal half of 10 or 5.
$2\frac{1}{2}$ symbols $= 20 + 5 = 25$ books

   Answer   25 books

c. ***Think!***   How many symbols follow Davin's name? The 1 symbol indicates that he read 10 books.
10 books $+ ? = 25$ books read by Jennifer

   Answer   15 books

Exercises

1. A group of children opened a lemonade stand. They sold each glass of lemonade for 10 cents each. Use the pictograph to answer Questions a through e about the lemonade sales.

GLASSES OF LEMONADE SOLD IN ONE WEEK
EACH ⊔ STANDS FOR 10 GLASSES

MONDAY	⊔ ⊔ ⊔
TUESDAY	⊔ ⊔ ⊔ ⊔
WEDNESDAY	⊔ ⊔ ⊔
THURSDAY	⊔ ⊔ ⊔ ⊔
FRIDAY	⊔ ⊔ ⊔ ⊔ ⊔
SATURDAY	⊔ ⊔ ⊔ ⊔ ⊔ ⊔ ⊔
SUNDAY	⊔ ⊔

LEMONADE
10¢

a. On which day were the most glasses of lemonade sold?

b. Lauren drank the unsold glasses of lemonade on Saturday. If 70 glasses of lemonade were prepared for Saturday, how many glasses did she drink?

c. On which two days were the most sales made?

d. On which day was the least amount of money made from sales?

*e. How much money was collected from the sales of the lemonade?

2. A balloon was given to each person attending a school carnival. Use the pictograph to answer Questions a through d.

DAY	CARNIVAL ATTENDANCE STANDS FOR 50 PEOPLE
FRIDAY	🎈🎈🎈🎈🎈
SATURDAY	🎈🎈🎈🎈🎈🎈🎈
SUNDAY	🎈🎈🎈🎈

a. On which day were 250 balloons given away?

b. How many people attended the carnival during the 3 days?

c. 400 balloons were prepared for Saturday. Were there enough balloons?

Activity: COIN DROP

Purpose   To collect data and record it as a pictograph.

Materials   1 gallon (4 liter) jar   paper
egg holder or cup   pencil
10 coins

Procedure

- Center the egg holder in the bottom of the jar.
- Fill the jar with water.
- Hold one coin at a time above the water's surface.
- Drop each coin so that it falls through the water and into the egg holder.
- Use 10 coins for each turn.

- Draw a pictograph on the paper. Record the number of coins that fall into the egg holder during 10 turns, using a circle to represent each coin in the holder.

TURN	COINS DROPPED IN HOLDER ○ STANDS FOR ONE COIN
1	
2	EXAMPLE
3	
4	

Results   The coins fall straight down through the air and flip to the side when they hit the water's surface. A position above the water can be found to allow more coins to fall into the egg holder.

Turn	Coins Dropped in Holder ◯ Stands for one coin.
1	
2	
3	
4	
5	
6	
7	
8	
9	
10	

Did You Know?

Light changes direction when it enters water, as did the coins. This change in the direction of light is called refraction and causes objects in water to appear to be where they are not.

Solutions

1. a. *Think!*   Which day has the largest number of glass symbols?

   Answer   Saturday

   b. *Think!*   Find the difference between the number of glasses prepared and the number of glasses sold. How many were sold? How many prepared? prepared (70) – sold (65) = 5 glasses

   Answer   Lauren drank 5 glasses of lemonade.

   c. *Think!*   Which two days have the most symbols?

   Answer   Friday and Saturday

   d. *Think!*   On which day were the least sales made? This will be the day the least amount of money was made.

   Answer   Sunday

   *e. *Think!*   How many total glasses were sold? Count all of the symbols and multiply by the cost of one glass, 10 cents. 26 symbols $\times$ 10 = 260

   260 glasses $\times$ \$0.10 = \$26.00

   Answer   \$26.00

2. a. *Think!*   Number of people - Number of balloons
   ? symbols $\times$ 50 = 250
   ? = 5 symbols

   Thus, the day having 5 balloon symbols is the day that 250 balloons were given away.

   Answer   Friday

b. *Think!*   ? balloon symbols $\times$ 50 = Total attendance
16×50 = 800 people

Answer   800 people attended the carnival.

c. *Think!*   How many people received balloons on Saturday?
7 symbols $\times$ 50 = 350 people
400 balloons $-$ 350 balloons = 50 balloons

Answer   Yes, there were 50 extra balloons.

24
Circle Graph

Purpose   To interpret information on a circle graph.

Facts   Information on circle graphs is usually shown as a percentage. The larger the area of the graph used, the greater the percentage represented. The whole circle represents 100 percent or the total amount. Dividing the circle in half makes each section equal to 50 percent, and four equal divisions produce 25 percent portions.

Percentage is a special ratio that compares a number to 100. The percent symbol, %, means hundredths. 60% is read as "sixty percent" and means $^{60}/_{100}$, sixty hundredths. Percent numbers can be expressed as a decimal number by dividing the numerator by 100. Thus 60% is the same as $^{60}/_{100}$ or .60.

Problems

Question   **1.** Twenty children were asked about their favorite snacks. Find the number of children that ate each type of food.

a.   35% like potato chips

b.   60% like candy

c.   5% like raisins

a.   ***Think!*** $35\% = {}^{35}/_{100} = .35$
         35% of 20 children $= .35 \times 20 = 7$ children

     Answer   7 children like potato chips

b.   ***Think!*** $60\% = {}^{60}/_{100} = .60$
         60% of 20 children $= .60 \times 20 = 12$ children

     Answer   12 children like candy

c.   ***Think!*** $5\% = {}^{5}/_{100} = .05$
         5% of 20 children $= .05 \times 20 = 1$ child

     Answer   1 child likes raisins

Note: The sum of the number of children who like the different snacks is equal to 20, the total number of children.

2. Use the circle graph to answer Questions 1 through 3 about the 12 liters of air inside the balloon.

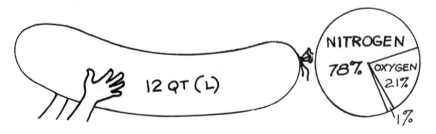

a.   What is the sum of all the percentages in the graph?

b.   What percentage of the air in the balloon is nitrogen?

c.   How many liters of oxygen gas are in the balloon?

a.   *Think!*   78% + 21% + 1% = 100%

Answer   100% is the sum of all the percentages in any circle graph.

b.   *Think!*   Find the part of the circle labeled nitrogen.

Answer   78%

c.   *Think!*   21% of the volume of air in the balloon is oxygen.
                       thus
                       21% of 12 qt (12 liters) = .21 × 12 qt
                                                = 2.52 qt (2.52 liters)

Answer   2.52 qt (2.52 liters) of oxygen in the balloon

Exercises

1. The circle graph shows the percentage of hair color in a class of 30 students. Use the graph to determine how many students have each hair color.

a. brown

b. blond

c. black

d. red

2. Davin divided his daily homework time of 60 minutes. Use the graph to determine how many minutes he now spends on the separate subjects.

a. math

b. art

c. history

d. science

e. spelling

*3. The circle graph is a record of how Ryan spends his time in a 24-hour day.

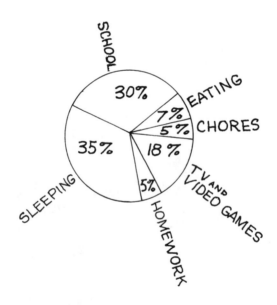

a. How much sleep does Ryan get each week?

b. How much time does he spend studying if he only studies on week nights?

Activity: COLOR WHEEL

Purpose   To use a circle graph of colors to demonstrate blending of colors.

Materials   cardboard   ruler
tempera paints, red, blue, and yellow   pencil
paint brush   glue
straight pin

Procedure

■ Cut an 8 in. (20 cm) diameter circle from the stiff paper.

■ Use the pencil to draw lines to divide the paper circle into three equal parts. Each part represents 33 1/3%.

■ Color each section of the circle a different color, red, blue, and yellow.

■ Allow the paint to dry.

■ Use the pin to make two holes in the center of the circle about 1/2 in. (1 cm) apart.

■ Cut a 24 in. (60 cm) length of string.

■ Run the string through one of the holes and back through the other one.

■ Tie the ends of the string together.

■ Move the paper circle to the center of the string.

■ Turn the circle around until the string is tightly twisted.

■ Pull outward on both ends of the string until it starts to unwind, then release the tension on the string so that it winds in the opposite direction.

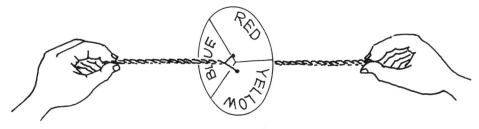

■ Continue to pull and release the string causing the circle to quickly spin back and forth.

Results   The paper circle quickly spins back and forth. The colors blend together and a grayish color is seen.

Did You Know?

Your brain retains each color ¹/₁₆ of a second after the section has passed, causing a blending of the colors seen. If the colors used to paint the paper were pure blue, red, and yellow, the color of the spinning paper would be white instead of grey.

Solutions

1. a. *Think!*   40% of 30 children = number with brown hair
40% × 30 = .40 × 30 = 12 children

Answer   12 children with brown hair

b. *Think!*   30% of 30 children = number with blond hair
30% × 30 = .30 × 30 = 9 children

Answer   9 children with blond hair

c. *Think!*   20% of 30 children = number with black hair
20% × 30 = .20 × 30 = 6 children

Answer   6 children with black hair

d. *Think!*   10% of 30 children = number with red hair
10% × 30 = .10 × 30 = 3 children

Answer   3 children with red hair

2. a. *Think!* $10\% \times 60$ minutes = study time for math
$10\% \times 60 = .10 \times 60 = 6$ minutes

Answer   6 minutes study time for math

b. *Think!* $25\% \times 60$ minutes = study time for art
$25\% \times 60 = .25 \times 60 = 15$ minutes

Answer   15 minutes study time for art

c. *Think!* $20\% \times 60$ minutes = study time for history
$20\% \times 60 = .20 \times 60 = 12$ minutes

Answer   12 minutes study time for history

d. *Think!* $15\% \times 60$ minutes = study time for science
$15\% \times 60 = .15 \times 60 = 9$ minutes

Answer   9 minutes study time for science

e. *Think!* $30\% \times 60$ minutes = study time for spelling
$30\% \times 60 = .30 \times 60 = 18$ minutes

Answer   18 minutes study time for spelling

*3. a. *Think!*   There are 7 days in a week. Multiply the time spent in sleep in 1 day by 7.
$35\% \times 24$ hours $= .35 \times 24$ hours $= 8.4$ hours
8.4 hours $\times 7 = 58.8$ hours per week

Answer   58.8 hours of sleep each week

b. *Think!*   Weekdays are Monday through Friday, thus he studies 5 days each week.
$5\% \times 24$ hours $= .05 \times 24 = 1.2$ hours
1.2 hours $\times 5 = 6$ hours per week

Answer   6 hours of studying each week

25
Graphs

Purpose   To use data charts to construct graphs.

Facts   Each division on the graph must have the same value. The vertical and horizontal scales are labeled to indicate what they measure. A title explains what is being graphed. The type of graph depends on the data collected. When one factor varies while a second factor changes, such as the sale of the cookies each day in the example, a line graph would best represent the data. Bar graphs are used to show comparisons between data. Circle graphs best represent fractions, and percentages and pictographs can be used as score cards or when large quantities are involved. Graph paper makes constructing a graph easier since the squares are uniform.

Problem

Question   Use the following Girl Scout Cookie Sales data chart to construct a line graph.

Girl Scout Cookie Sales	
Day	Number of Cases Sold
Monday	10
Tuesday	20
Wednesday	30
Thursday	20
Friday	35

Graphs A and B use the same value for the scales, but the position of the information is different. A line graph is used when one factor varies while the second factor changes. The days change while the sales vary. Placing the factor that varies on the vertical scale as on graph A produces a graph that is easier to interpret.

Graphs C and D show how the size of the scale can affect the appearance of the graph. Graph D has larger spaces between the vertical scale measurements than the horizontal measurements, and so the graph makes the changes in sales appear steeper or larger.

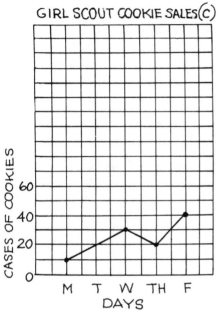

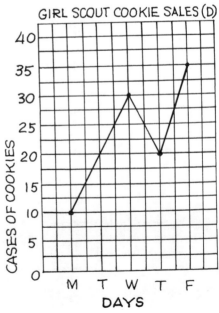

Exercises

1. Use the following data chart to construct a line graph. The variable number of calls are to be on the vertical scale. Be sure to label the vertical and horizontal scales and give the graph a title.

Emergency Calls	
Time	Calls Received
6 A.M.	65
8 A.M.	70
10 A.M.	80
12 NOON	90
2 P.M.	95
4 P.M.	95
6 P.M.	90

2. Construct a bar graph to record the information about the types and numbers of classroom pets. Use the horizontal scale for the number of pets and be sure to start at 0.

Classroom Pets	
Pet	Number
White mice	4
Hamsters	2
Guinea pigs	3
Guppies	10
Snake	1

*3. Construct a circle graph to represent the number of each color of beads.

Bead Color	
Color	Number
Red	8
Blue	16
Green	24
Yellow	4
Orange	12

Activity: **RING THE BOTTLE**

Purpose   To use a graph to record the score for a game.

Materials   ruler   glass soda bottle
scissors   paper
pencil   ring for a canning jar
string   players

Procedure

■ Cut a 24 in. (60 cm) length of string.

■ Tie one end of the string to the end of the pencil and the opposite end of the string to the ring.

■ Stand the soda bottle on the floor.

■ Hold the free end of the pencil and dangle the ring above the top of the soda bottle.

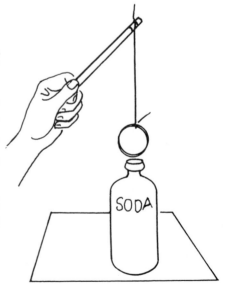

■ Lower the string, placing the ring over the bottle.

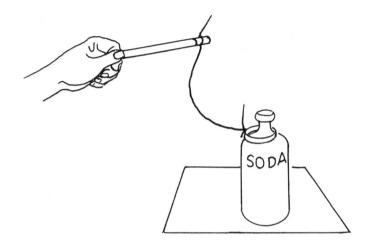

■ Ten attempts to place the ring over the bottle is considered as one turn.

■ Prepare a pictograph score card. Use a bottle or a symbol of your choice to represent ringing the bottle on the pictograph score card.

PLAYERS	RING THE BOTTLE SCORECARD
	🥏 STANDS FOR ONE RING OVER THE BOTTLE
CAROL	🥏 🥏
KATE	🥏 🥏
AMBER	🥏
KRYSTI	🥏 🥏 🥏

EXAMPLE

Results   The pictograph score card method makes it easy to decide who is the winner of the game.

Did You Know?

A pictograph using an X to represent 10 points is often used by domino players. Half of the X, a single slash, indicates 5 points. Examples of using this method are:

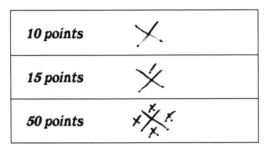

10 points	
15 points	
50 points	

Solutions

1. Though there was no time with 0 calls, the vertical scale starts at 0 calls. There is a better comparison when the vertical scale begins at zero.

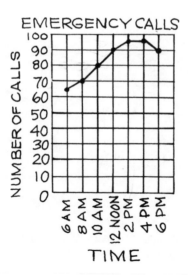

2.

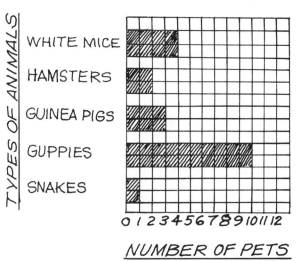

CLASSROOM PETS

TYPES OF ANIMALS

WHITE MICE

HAMSTERS

GUINEA PIGS

GUPPIES

SNAKES

0 1 2 3 4 5 6 7 8 9 10 11 12

NUMBER OF PETS

3. *Think!* What is the total number of beads?
8 + 16 + 24 + 4 + 12 = 64

What is the smallest number? 4
4 × ? = 64
? = 16

Divide the circle into 16 parts and each part will be equal to 4 beads.

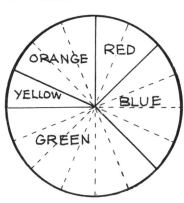

IV
Geometry

26
Angles

Purpose   To name and identify right, acute, and obtuse angles.

Facts   A **ray** is a straight line with one endpoint. An **angle** is formed when two rays have the same endpoint. The endpoint is called the **vertex**. Three letters are used to name an angle with the vertex as the center letter. Each angle has two names and either can be correctly used. The names of the angle below are: angle ABC or angle CBA. The word angle can be replaced by the symbol for the word angle, $\angle$. The names of the angle are thus $\angle$ ABC or $\angle$ CBA.

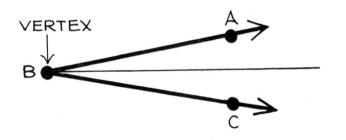

The unit of measure for an angle is a degree. One degree is written as $1°$.

A **right angle** measures $90°$ and forms a square corner. A small square is used to indicate a right angle. An **acute angle** is any angle that measures less than $90°$. An **obtuse angle** is any angle that measures greater than $90°$.

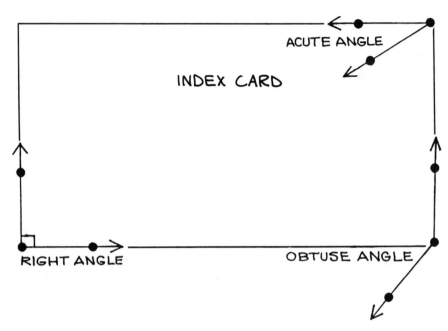

An index card can be used to identify the different angles. Place the card inside the angle so that one edge lies on a ray and the corner of the card points the angle's vertex. A right angle has both rays in line with the edge of the card. An acute angle has one ray under the card. An obtuse angle has one ray pointing away from the card.

Problem

Question   Use an index card to identify each angle as right, acute, or obtuse.

a.

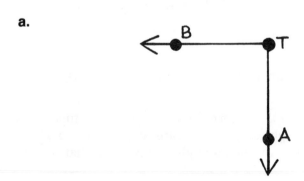

b.

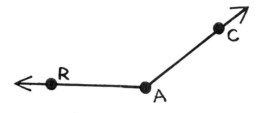

c.

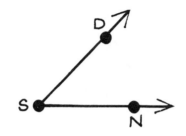

a.   ∠BTA or ∠ATB, right angle

b.   ∠RAC or ∠CAR, obtuse angle

c.   ∠DSN or ∠NSD, acute angle

Exercises

1. Use an index card to identify each angle as right, acute, or obtuse.

   a.

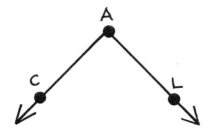

b.

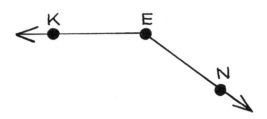

c.

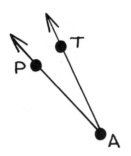

d.

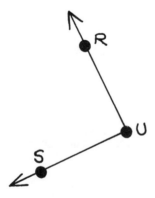

2. Draw an example for each of the angles.

    a. ∠KIM, a right angle

    b. ∠RED, an acute angle

    c. ∠MEG, an obtuse angle

3. Find the number of right, acute, and obtuse angles formed by the sides of this irregular-shaped figure.

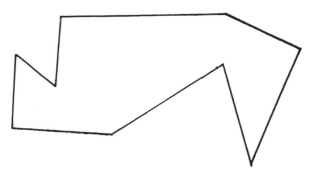

Activity: PUSH

Purpose To demonstrate how the angle of a boat's bow affects its movement.

Materials cookie sheet   toothpick
stiff paper, use a file folder dish soap
ruler   pencil
scissors   two helpers

Procedure

■ Draw three triangles about 1 in. (2½ cm) high on the stiff paper.

■ The top of one triangle is to be a right angle; the top of the second angle is to be acute; and the top of the third angle is to be obtuse.

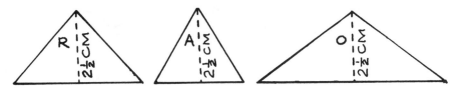

■ A small notch is to be cut out of the base of each triangular-shaped boat.

■ Fill the cookie sheet with water.

■ Space the paper boats on the surface of the water at the edge of the pan.

■ Moisten the tips of three toothpicks with dish soap and give one to each of your two helpers.

■ Each of you is to touch the water inside the notch of a triangle boat with the wet toothpick.

■ Observe the movement of the boats.

Results   The paper boats blast across the surface of the water. The boat with the acute angle should be the fastest boat and the obtuse boat the slowest.

Did You Know?

The bow of a boat is pointed to allow it to easily move through the water. Cars are designed to cut through the air as they move, while large trucks often have a high, curved shield attached to divert the air up and away. The less air and water resistance for the cars, trucks, and boats, the less fuel needed to move the vehicle. This is one small way to be environmentally savvy.

Solutions

1. **a.** Right angle

   b. Obtuse angle

c. Acute angle

d. Right angle

2. a.

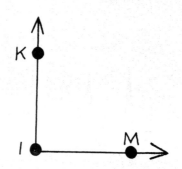

b.

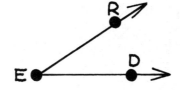

c.

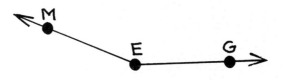

3.

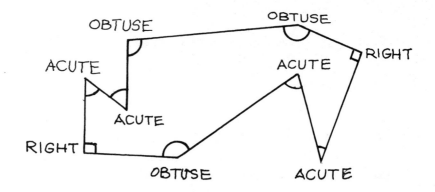

27
Protractor

Purpose   To measure angles using a protractor.

Facts   A **protractor** is an instrument used to measure angles in degrees. It is shaped like a half-circle. To measure an angle with a protractor, place the center mark of the instrument on the vertex of the angle and the edge on one ray of the angle. There will be two numbers to choose from where the second ray crosses the scale. One of the numbers will represent an acute angle (one that is less than 90°), and the other will be obtuse (more than 90°). The sum of these two numbers will always equal 180°. The ray IK crosses the scale at 50° and 130°. Since the angel is acute, ∠ KIM is 50°.

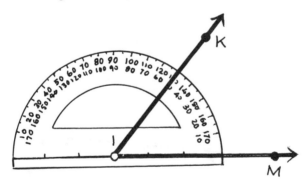

A sheet of paper or any straight edge can be used when angles have rays too short to cross the scale of the protractor. Lay the edge of the paper along the ray and read the numbers where the paper crosses the scale of the protractor. In the diagram, the edge of the paper crosses at angles 40° and 140°. Angle JAM is obtuse, so JAM is 140°.

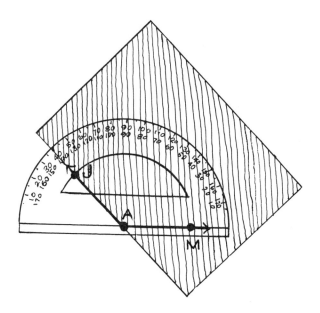

Problem

Question   Use a protractor to measure the angles in diagrams A
and B.

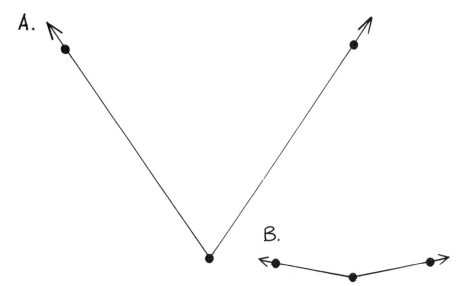

a. *Think!*   The angle is acute (less than 90°). Which of the
angles choices, 110° or 70°, is acute?

Answer   70°

b. *Think!*   The angle is obtuse (greater than 90°). Which of
the angle choices, 160° or 20°, is obtuse?

Answer   160°

Exercises

1. Use a protractor to measure the angles.

a.

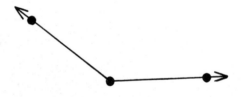

b.

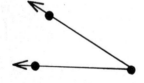

c.

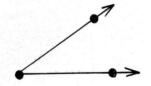

*2. The face of a clock can be used to give direction. If straight ahead is defined as North and the large hand points to the hour of 12, what is the direction for these times?

a. 2 o'clock

b. 3 o'clock

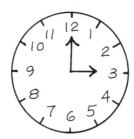

c. 7 o'clock

Activity: SUN CLOCK

Purpose   To use a protractor to compare the angles on a clock with those on a sun clock.

Materials   piece of cardboard, about 8 in. (20 cm) square
protractor   marking pen
pencil   watch

Procedure

- Place the protractor on a piece of cardboard.

- Use the marking pen to draw around the outside of the protractor.

- Mark the positions of these angles on the cardboard:
  0°, 30°, 60°, 90°, 120°, 150°, 180°.

- Turn the protractor around and mark around the outside of the protractor to complete the circle.

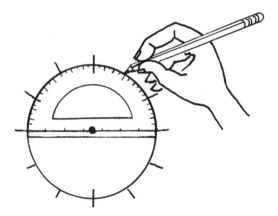

- Mark the positions of these angles on the cardboard:
  30°, 60°, 90°, 120°, 150°.

- Write the numbers 1 through 12 on the inside of the circle as they appear on the face of a clock. Position each number beneath one of the marked angles.

- Place the cardboard on the ground with the clock diagram facing up. Be sure the clock will be in direct sunlight.

- Insert the point of the pencil through the center of the clock and into the ground. The pencil must stand straight up and down.

- When your watch reads 1:00, rotate the cardboard around the pencil so that the shadow of the pencil falls across the number 1 on the circle. (Set your watch back 1 hour if you are doing this during daylight saving time.)

- At 2, 3, 4, and 5 o'clock, mark and number the pencil's shadow.

- Use the protractor to measure the angles between each hour on the clock and between the shadow marks for each hour.

Results   The numbers on the clock are 30° apart, but the numbers on the sun clock, formed by the pencil's shadow, are all different. The changing position of the sun causes the angles between the pencil's shadow to change.

Did You Know?

The sun is not moving across the sky as it appears to do from morning to night. Instead the sun is stationary while the earth rotates on its axis toward the east.

Solutions

1. a. Think!   The angle is obtuse (greater than 90°). Which of the angle choices, 40° or 140°, is obtuse?

Answer   140°

b. *Think!*   The angle is acute (less than 90°). Which of the angle choices, 30° or 150°, is acute?

Answer   30°

c. *Think!*   The angle is acute and touches the fifth mark between the numbered divisions. The angle choices are 35° and 145°. Which of these choices is an acute angle?

Answer   35°

2. a. *Think!*   What are the angle choices? 60° and 120°. Is the angle acute or obtuse? Acute. Is the angle to the right or left of 12? Right.

Answer   60° to the right

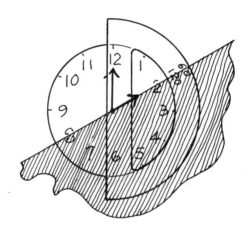

b. *Think!*   What is the angle? 90° Is the angle to the right or left of 12? Right.

Answer   90° to the right

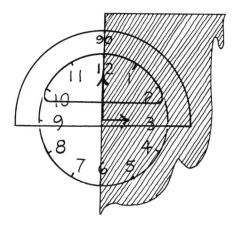

c. *Think!* What are the angle choices? 30° and 150°. Is the angle obtuse or acute? Obtuse. Is the angle to the right or left of 12? Left.

Answer 150° to the left

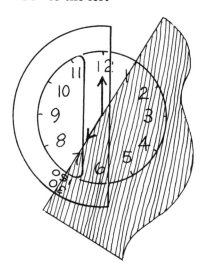

28
Using a Protractor

Purpose   To use a protractor to determine the height of distant objects.

Facts   A protractor is used in constructing an **astrolabe**, which is an instrument used to measure the heights of distant objects. In the starting position, the weighted string hangs straight down, passing over the 90° mark on the protractor scale. Tilting one end of the protractor moves the scale, but the string continues to hang straight down. The angle of the raised protractor and the Height Chart are used to determine the height of the distant object. An average height of a person using the astrolabe and an object at a distance of 100 ft (31 m) were used to determine the heights in the Astrolabe Height Chart.

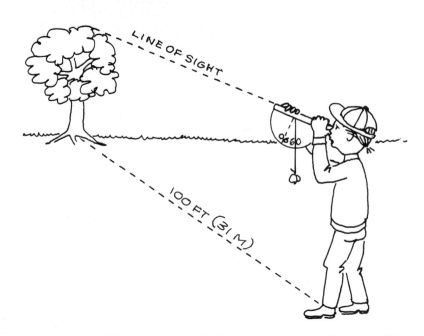

Astrolabe Height Chart

Angle in Degrees	Height in Feet	Height in Meters
1	1.75	.54
2	3.52	1.08
3	5.24	1.61
4	6.99	2.15
5	8.75	2.69
10	17.63	5.43
15	26.79	8.24
20	36.40	11.20
25	46.63	14.35
30	57.74	17.76
35	70.02	21.54
40	83.91	25.82
45	100.00	31
50	119.18	36.67
55	142.81	43.94
60	173.21	53.29
65	214.45	65.98
70	274.74	84.54
75	373.21	114.83
80	567.13	174.50
85	1143.00	351.94

Problem

Question   Use the readings from the astrolabe and the Astrolabe Height Chart to determine the height of the tree.

Think!   On what degree did the string start?   90°

On what degree did the string stop?   60°

What is the difference between the starting and stopping position of the string? $90° - 60° = 30°$

What is the height at 30°?

Answer   57.74 ft (17.76 m)

Exercises

The starting position for the astrolabe in each problem is 90°. Use the reading on the astrolabe scale and the Astrolabe Height Chart to determine the height of the distant object in each problem.

1. What is the height of the flagpole?

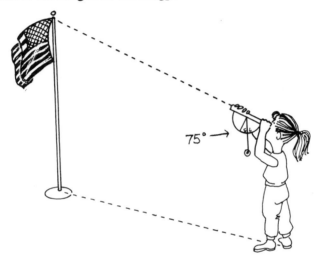

2. How high is the rocket from the ground?

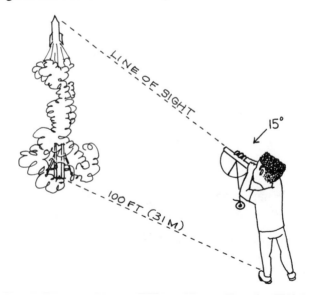

*3. The tightrope is 113.33 ft (34.87 m) from the ground. Use the astrolabe measurement to determine the height of the man walking on the rope.

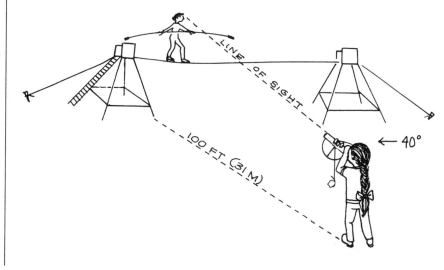

Activity: ASTROLABE

Purpose   To use an astrolabe to determine the height of objects.

Materials   drinking straw   washer
               protractor   yard or meter stick
               string   helper

Procedure

■ Cut a 12 in. (30 cm) length of string.

■ Tie the string to the center of the protractor and attach the washer to the free end of the string.

■ Tape the straw to the top edge of the protractor.

■ Stand 100 ft (31 m) from a tall object such as a tree or building. Use the measuring stick to measure the 100 ft (31 m) distance.

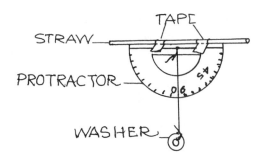

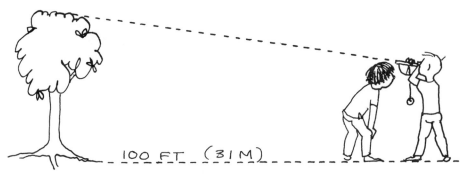

■ Look through the straw at the top of the object and have your helper determine the angle of the hanging string.

■ Use the Astrolabe Height Chart to determine the height of the object.

Results   The angle increases as the height of the object increases.

Did You Know?

The washer continues to hang straight down while the protractor rotates because of the pull of gravity. The gravity acting on the washer is a force that pulls it toward the center of the earth.

Solutions

1. Think!   On what degree did the string start?   90°

On what degree did the string stop?   75°

What is the difference between the starting and stopping positions of the string?   90° − 75° = 15°

What is the height at 15°?

Answer 26.79 ft (8.24 m) is the height of the flagpole.

1. Think! On what degree did the string start?   90°

On what degree did the string stop?   15°

What is the difference between the starting and stopping positions of the string?   90°-15° = 75°

What is the height at 75°?

Answer 373.21 ft (114.83 m) is the height of the rocket.

3. Think! On what degree did the string start?   90°

On what degree did the string stop?   40°

What is the difference between the starting and stopping positions of the string?   90° − 40° = 50°

What is the height at 50°?   119.18 ft (36.67 m)

What is the difference between the height of the man on the rope and the height of the rope?

119.18 ft − 113.33 ft. = 5.85 ft
36.67 m − 34.87 m   = 1.8 m

Answer 5.85 ft (1.8 m) is the height of the man.

29
Polygons

Purpose To identify polygons.

Facts A **polygon** is a simple closed figure formed by straight lines. The sides of the polygon meet to form angles. The point where the sides meet is called a **vertex**.

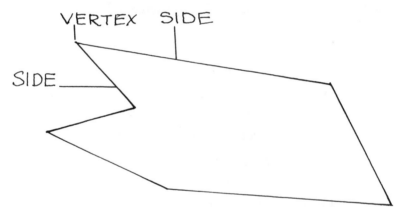

Polygons are named according to the number of sides in the structure. Some of the smaller and more common polygons are:

Name	Number of Sides
Triangle	3
Quadrilateral	4
Pentagon	5
Hexagon	6
Heptagon	7
Octagon	8
Nonagon	9
Decagon	10

Problem

Question   For each structure, determine:

    a. The number of straight sides.

    b. Is it a polygon?

    c. If it is a polygon, what kind of polygon.

1. **a.** No straight sides

    b. It is not a polygon.

2. **a.** No straight sides

    b. It is not a polygon.

3. **a.** 8 straight sides

    b. Yes, it is a polygon.

    c. Octagon

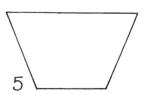

4. **a.** 3 straight sides

    b. Yes, it is a polygon.

    c. Triangle

5. **a.** 4 straight sides

    b. Yes, it is a polygon.

    c. Quadrilateral

Exercises

1. Name these common polygons.

2. For each structure A through G, determine:

a. The number of straight sides.

b. Is it a polygon?

c. The name of the polygon.

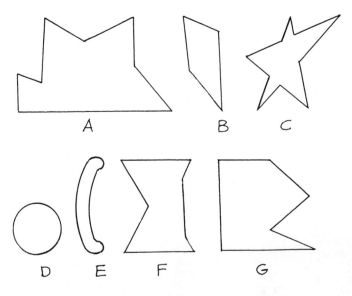

3. Study the shapes of these creatures and identify those from the indicated group that are from the imaginary planet of Zurp.

These creatures are from Zurp.

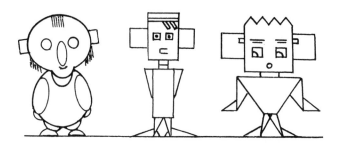

These creatures are not from Zurp.

Which of these creatures are from Zurp?

 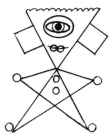 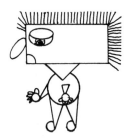

Activity: THREE TO FOUR

Purpose   To change the shape of polygons.

Materials   typing paper   scissors
                  marking pen

Procedure

- Fold 1 sheet of paper by placing a short end against a longer side.
- Use the scissors to cut the rectangle from the end of the paper.

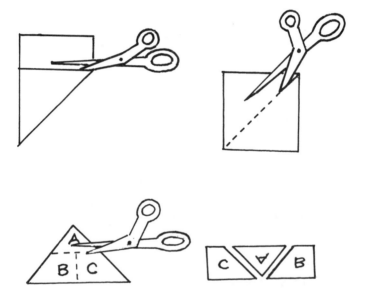

- Open the paper and cut across the diagonal fold. Use only one of the identical triangles that result from the cutting.
- Use the marking pen to mark a line along the edge of the triangle.
- Cut across the center of the triangle to form triangle A as seen in the diagram.
- Cut the resulting quadrilateral polygon in half to produce sections B and C.

- Position sections A, B, and C as shown to form a quadrilateral polygon.

- Rearrange the sections to form different polygons.

Results   The triangle is cut and arranged to form a rectangle, a quadrilateral polygon. Many different types of polygons can be formed with the three pieces.

Did You Know?

The sum of the angles in any triangle equals 180°. The three vertices from the triangle in this activity form a straight line, 180°, when placed together.

Solutions

1. a. A six-sided nut is an example of a hexagon.

   b. The pattern on soccer balls is that of a pentagon.

   c. The banner is a triangle.

2. A. a. 8 sides

   b. Yes

   c. Octagon

   B. a. 4 sides

   b. Yes

   c. Quadrilateral

C. a. 10 sides

   b. Yes

   c. Decagon

D. Not a polygon

E. Not a polygon

F. a. 7 sides

   b. Yes

   c. Heptagon

G. a. 6 sides

   b. Yes

   c. Hexagon

3. Zurps have square ears.

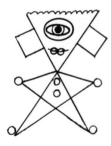 is the only Zurp.

30
Symmetry

Purpose   To identify lines of symmetry in a geometric figure.

Facts   A **symmetric figure** can be folded along a line of symmetry and the two halves of the figure fit exactly on each other. The **line of symmetry** divides the figure into two parts that are mirror images of each other. If a mirror is placed on the line of symmetry, the whole figure can be seen.

Some figures have more than one line of symmetry as indicated by the two lines on the diagram of the star. The butterfly has only one line of symmetry.

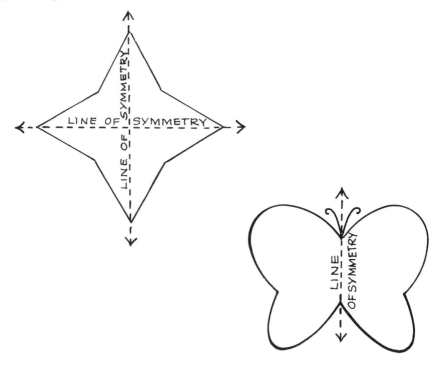

Problem

Question

Determine if the dotted lines are lines of symmetry for the figures.

a.

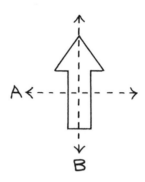

b.

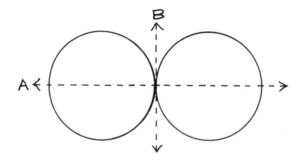

a.	*Think!*	On which line can the figure be folded to form two halves that exactly fit together?
	Answer	Line B
b.	*Think!*	On which lines can the figure be folded to form two halves that exactly fit together?
	Answer	Lines A and B

Exercises

1. Determine if the dotted lines are lines of symmetry for the figures.

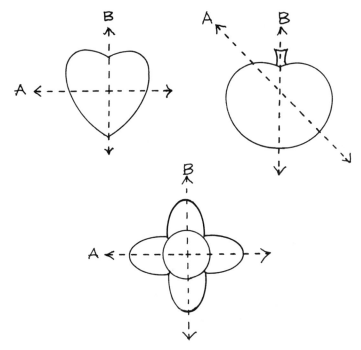

2. How many lines of symmetry does this octagon have?

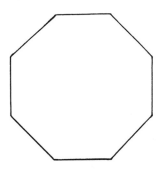

3. Take 4 sheets of paper. Fold each sheet once. On each, draw, then make a cut so that the piece has the shape when unfolded of one of these capital letters:

A, C, E, H

Activity: CUT OUTS

Purpose To cut out symmetrical figures.

Materials typing paper   scissors
pencil   colored marking pens

Procedure

- Fold over about 1 in. (2½ cm) of the end of 1 sheet of the paper.
- Turn the paper over and again fold the end over.
- Continue folding the ends back and forth until the entire sheet is folded like a fan.
- Flatten the folded sheet of paper.
- Use the pencil to draw half of a person on the folded paper. The left edge of the folded sheet will be the line of symmetry.
- Be sure to draw the arm out to the edge of the paper.
- Use the scissors to cut along the dotted lines. Be sure not to cut down the folded sides.

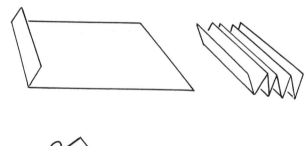

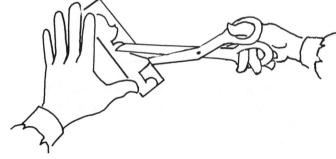

■ Unfold the paper.

■ Use the colored marking pens to add clothes and faces to the string of paper children.

Results   Cutting half of a child on lines of symmetry produces a whole person. The end of the arm is also placed along a folded line of symmetry, forming a string of identical children with linking arms.

Did You Know?

Placing a mirror along the center of your face results in a whole image of your face, but the observer may be surprised to discover a new you, since your real face is not symmetrical.

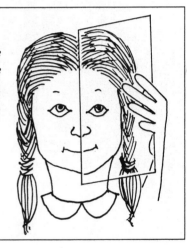

Solutions

1. a. *Think!*   On which line can the figure be folded to form two halves that exactly fit together?

Answer   Line B

b. *Think!*   On which line can the figure be folded to form two halves that exactly fit together?

Answer   Line B

c. *Think!*   On which lines can the figure be folded to form two halves that exactly fit together?

Answer   Lines A and B

2. The octagon has 8 lines of symmetry.

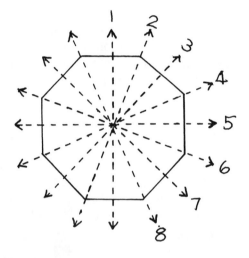

3. Patterns for cutting out letters.

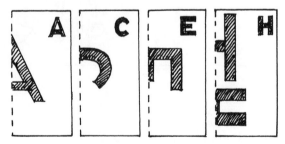

31
Reflections

Purpose   To identify mirror images.

Facts   A line of symmetry divides a figure into two halves that would fit exactly on each other if folded along the line. The edge of a mirror acts like a line of symmetry between the real object and the reflected image. The real object and the reflected image would fit exactly on each other if a fold could be made at the edge of the mirror.

Problem

Question

1. Do diagrams a and b show mirror images?

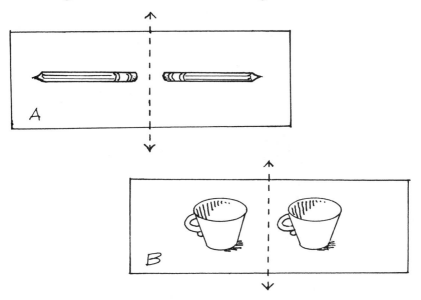

>   ***Think!*** Will the two halves match if the picture is folded along
>   the dotted line?
>
>   **Answer** Yes, the pencils are mirror images, but the cups are *not*
>   mirror images.

Exercises

1. Are diagrams a through c mirror images?

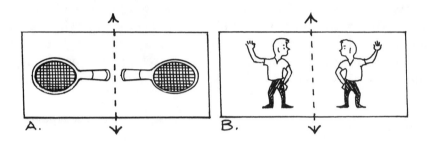

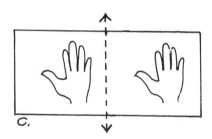

2. Placing a mirror along the dotted line completes the figure. Select
the correct mirror image for the drawing.

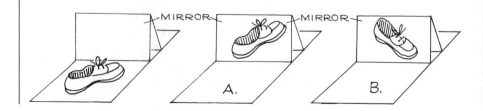

*3. Predict the resulting figure if a mirror is placed along the dotted line.

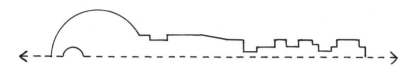

Activity: **MIRROR IMAGES**

Purpose   To determine the direction of mirror images.

Materials   shoe box   writing paper
masking tape   pencil
flat mirror

Procedure

- Use the tape to secure the mirror to the side of the shoe box.

- Place a sheet of paper under the edge of the mirror.

- Use the pencil to print your name on the paper.

- Observe the direction of the letter seen in the mirror.

- Place a clean sheet of paper under the mirror's edge.

- Print your name on the paper so that the image in the mirror looks correct.

Results Mirror images are backwards. Left is right and right is left. The letters appear to be upside down because the paper is placed at an angle to the mirror. If you fold the paper at the edge of the mirror and raise it upward, the writing and the mirror image would exactly fit on each other.

Did You Know?

You have never seen yourself as others see you. Looking into a mirror always gives you a reversed image.

Solutions

1. Think! Will the two halves match if the picture is folded along the dotted line?

Answer *a.* Yes, the tennis rackets are mirror images.

b. Yes, the figures are mirror images.

c. No, both are right hands and are not mirror images.

2. Think! If a fold could be made at the edge of the mirror, which reflected image would match the real object?

Answer B

3. A key

Glossary

Acute angle: Any angle that measures less than 90°.

Angle: Two rays that have the same endpoint form an angle.

Area: The amount of surface inside a structure.

Astrolabe: Instrument used to measure the heights of distant objects.

Celsius (C): The name of the metric system of measuring temperature.

Chord: A line segment whose endpoints are on a circle.

Circumference: The distance around a circle.

Common factor: One number that will divide evenly into the numerator and denominator.

Condensation: The change from a gas to a liquid.

Congruent figures: Geometric figures that are the same size and shape.

Degree (angle): A unit for measuring angles.

Degree (temperature): A temperature unit.

Denominator: The bottom number in a fraction. It tells the number of equal parts in the whole unit.

Diameter: A chord that passes through the center of a circle.

End point: The end of a line segment.

Equivalent fractions: Fractions that stand for the same amount.

Evaporation: The change from a liquid to a gas.

Factor(s):   Numbers that are multiplied to form a product. Example: In $2 \times 5 = 10$, 2 and 5 are factors.

Fahrenheit: The name of the English system of measuring temperature.

Friction: A resistance to movement.

Gravity: The downward pull on all objects.

Half-life: The time it takes for half of a radioactive material to change, to disintegrate, or become nonradioactive.

Kilometer: Metric unit for measuring distance. 1.6 km equals 1 mile.

Line of symmetry: A line that divides a figure into two parts that match if the figure is folded along the line.

Mass: The amount of matter in an object.

Numerator: The top number in a fraction. It tells how many equal parts are being considered.

Obtuse angle: Any angle that measures greater than 90°.

Perimeter: The distance around the outside of a plane figure.

Pi (π):   The ratio of the circumference of a circle to its diameter. When rounded to the nearest hundredth, pi equals 3.14.

Polygon: A simple closed figure whose sides are straight lines.

Product: The result of multiplication.

Protractor: An instrument used to measure angles.

Psychrometer: An instrument used to measure relative humidity.

Quadrilateral: Polygon with four sides.

Quotient: The result of division.

Radius: A straight line that connects the center of a circle to any point on the outside of the circle.

Ray: A straight line with one endpoint.

Rectangle: Four-sided figure with four right angles.

Relative humidity: The amount of water vapor in the air.

Refraction: Change in the direction of light.

Right angle: An angle that measures $90°$.

Square: Rectangle with congruent sides and $90°$ angles in all four corners.

Sum: The answer to addition.

Surface area: The total outside area of an object.

Symmetric figure: A figure that, when folded along a line of symmetry, has two halves that superimpose exactly on each other.

Triangle: A three-sided figure in one plane.

Vertex: The common endpoint of two or more rays to form angles.

Volume: The number of cubic units necessary to fill a three-dimensional figure.

Weight: The amount of pull that gravity has on an object.

Whole number: Any of the numbers 0, 1, 2, 3, 4, 5, 6, . . .

Index

Get these fun and exciting books by Janice VanCleave at your local bookstore, call toll-free 1-800-225-5945 or visit our Web site at: www.wiley.com/children/

Janice VanCleave's Science for Every Kid Series

____Astronomy	53573-7	$11.95 US / 15.95 CAN
____Biology	50381-9	$11.95 US / 15.95 CAN
____Chemistry	62085-8	$11.95 US / 15.95 CAN
____Constellations	15979-4	$12.95 US / 15.95 CAN
____Dinosaurs	30812-9	$10.95 US / 15.95 CAN
____Earth Science	53010-7	$11.95 US / 15.95 CAN
____Ecology	10086-2	$10.95 US / 15.95 CAN
____Geography	59842-9	$11.95 US / 15.95 CAN
____Geometry	31141-3	$11.95 US / 15.95 CAN
____Human Body	02408-2	$11.95 US / 15.95 CAN
____Math	54265-2	$12.95 US / 15.95 CAN
____Oceans	12453-2	$12.95 US / 15.95 CAN
____Physics	52505-7	$12.95 US / 15.95 CAN

Janice VanCleave's Spectacular Science Projects Series

____Animals	55052-3	$10.95 US / 12.95 CAN
____Earthquakes	57107-5	$10.95 US / 12.95 CAN
____Electricity	31010-7	$10.95 US / 12.95 CAN
____Gravity	55050-7	$10.95 US / 12.95 CAN
____Insects & Spiders	16396-1	$10.95 US / 15.50 CAN
____Machines	57108-3	$10.95 US / 12.95 CAN
____Magnets	57106-7	$10.95 US / 12.95 CAN
____Microscopes & Magnifying Lenses	58956-X	$10.95 US / 12.95 CAN
____Molecules	55054-X	$10.95 US / 12.95 CAN
____Plants	14687-0	$10.95 US / 12.95 CAN
____Rocks & Minerals	10269-5	$10.95 US / 12.95 CAN
____Volcanoes	30811-0	$10.95 US / 12.95 CAN
____Weather	03231-X	$10.95 US / 12.95 CAN

Janice VanCleave's Science Bonanzas Series

____200 Gooey, Slippery, Slimy, Weird & Fun Experiments
57921-1 $12.95 US / 16.95 CAN

____201 Awesome, Magical, Bizarre & Incredible Experiments
31011-5 $12.95 US / 16.95 CAN

____202 Oozing, Bubbling, Dripping & Bouncing Experiments
14025-2 $12.95 US / 16.95 CAN

Janice VanCleave's Play and Find Out About Science Series

____Play and Find Out About the Human Body
12935-6 $12.95 US / 18.50 CAN

____Play and Find Out About Nature
12940-2 $12.95 US / 16.95 CAN

____Play and Find Out About Math
12938-0 $12.95 US / 18.50 CAN

____Play and Find Out About Science
12941-0 $12.95 US / 16.95 CAN

Janice VanCleave's Guide to the Best Science Fair Projects

____Guide to the Best Science Fair Projects
14802-4 $14.95 US / 19.95 CAN

Janice VanCleave's A+ Projects for Young Adults Series

____Biology	58628-5	$12.95 US / 17.95 CAN
____Chemistry	58630-7	$12.95 US / 17.95 CAN

Prices subject to change without notice.